Books are to be returned on or before
the last date below.

n
n

LIBREX–

WITHDRAWN

LIVERPOOL JMU LIBRARY

3  1111  01335  2941

D0533121

**Other titles in the Education as a Humanitarian Response series**

*Education and Reconciliation*, Julia Paulson

*Education, Refugees and Asylum Seekers*, Lala Demirdjian

*Education, Aid and Aid Agencies*, Zuki Karpinska

**Also available from Continuum**

*Multiculturalism and Education*, Richard Race

*Comparative and International Education*, David Phillips, Michele Schweisfurth & Erwin Epstein

# Education
# as a Global
# Concern

## Colin Brock

### Education as Humanitarian Response

continuum

**Continuum International Publishing Group**
The Tower Building
11 York Road
London
SE1 7NX

80 Maiden Lane
Suite 704
New York
NY 10038

www.continuumbooks.com

© Colin Brock 2011

All rights reserved. No part of this publication may be reproduced or transmitted in any form or by any means, electronic or mechanical, including photocopying, recording, or any information storage or retrieval system, without prior permission in writing from the publishers.

Colin Brock has asserted his right under the Copyright, Designs and Patents Act, 1988, to be identified as Author of this work.

**British Library Cataloguing-in-Publication Data**
A catalogue record for this book is available from the British Library.

ISBN:   978-1-4411-3028-0 (paperback)
        978-1-4411-9296-7 (hardcover)

**Library of Congress Cataloging-in-Publication Data**
Brock, Colin.
  Education as a global concern / Colin Brock.
    p. cm. -- (Education as a Humanitarian Response)
  Includes index.
  ISBN 978-1-4411-3028-0 (pbk.) -- ISBN 978-1-4411-9296-7 (hardcover)
  1. Education and globalization. 2. International education. 3. International schools. I. Title. II. Series.

  LC191.B685 2011
  302.43'2--dc22

                                    2010028420


Typeset by Free Range Book Design & Production
Printed and bound in India by Replika Press Pvt Ltd

# Contents

# Acknowledgements

I would like to thank all those who have been of assistance in developing this book and the series as a whole, especially Alison Baker the Commissioning Editor for Education for Continuum and her team, and all the editors and contributors to the other volumes in the series.

As far as this book in particular is concerned I would like to thank especially Dr Jenny Hsieh for computing the figures for electronic transmission, and Shirley Anne Brock for compiling the index.

Any errors and shortcomings in this book are entirely my own responsibility.

Colin Brock

# Preface

This book is primarily for students, especially at undergraduate and masters levels. Its principal aim is to help engender a view of *education as a humanitarian response* that is not limited to the narrow context of disasters, but instead applied to all education.

It is also the introductory volume to a series under that same title. Each contributing volume focuses on a different issue or human group, such as: situations of conflict and post-conflict; aid and education; HIV/AIDS; refugees; and minorities. Others should follow. They are all illustrating and analysing humanitarian responses to educational needs. One of the aims of this book is to take the holistic approach that necessarily follows in such circumstances, and apply it to examining mainstream systems and the situation of the marginalized majority on and beyond their fringes.

Such a broad brush requires the illustration of issues with examples from various parts of the world. This in turn serves a secondary aim of this book, which is to challenge and extend conventional perspectives on education that in nearly all societies are notoriously introspective. Most people go through life with a view of formal education based on experiencing only one system, topped up with uninformed rumours and prejudices about others. The main purpose of *comparative and international education* is to enable one to gain other perspectives on one's own experience, so as to understand and critique it more effectively. Regrettably, due to the widespread introspection alluded to above, even among educationists, comparative education finds itself on the periphery. Even worse, along with the other fields comprising what is known as 'the foundations of education', such as the history of education, philosophy of education and economics of education, it is in danger of extinction. Most readers of this book are likely to be students of education or related social science disciplines. Hopefully the global perspectives encouraged here will help them to extend their horizons beyond the increasingly instrumental and managerial approach to educational studies that has become conventional.

This is not a textbook as such, but rather an invitation to think outside the box. Its aim is to challenge the conventional wisdom regarding education as a panacea for all ills: social, cultural, economic, political, technical and environmental. That is certainly what education is not. So we can make a start by trying to understand what education is. Is it schools? No, it is much more than that. Schooling, if you can get it – and many in the world cannot – is just part of education for part of the time of a small part of most people's lives. So schooling is part of a part of a part, which adds up to not very much, but crucially it is formative. On top of that schools are often blamed for all kinds of problems such as military or sporting defeat, criminality and antisocial behaviour, and lack of economic progress. That is the downside of being a panacea! Inevitably there are problems with schools, so should we 'de-school society' as Ivan Illich famously advocated in 1971? No we should not, because schools are a vital part of education; an essential element of it. In any case, they are not going to go away. But Illich did present a clue to a more accurate and holistic view of education when he speculated about the prospects for informal education and lifelong learning.

So where do we go from here? That is the question forming the title of the final chapter of this book. First we need to establish where we are at, what it's all about, and why there is a case for considering education to be a global concern.

Education is about learning, a quality not unique to human beings but one so massively more developed than in any other form of life that it essentially defines our humanity. But it is also a characteristic of humans not to learn. We can see this at many levels from the determined adolescent male underachiever, to the curious propensity of governments to adopt policies that have failed in the past or in other comparable countries. Many thousands of years after the emergence of *homo sapiens*, why has the wisdom embodied in that designation not advanced to the same degree as our technical expertise? Clearly, the epithet 'sapiens' has turned out to be wildly optimistic and self-congratulatory. We have certainly made massive progress in technical and instrumental terms, ranging from the control and even eradication of major diseases through instant intercontinental communication to the legal regulation of human behaviour. Yet we are on the verge of destroying the ecological survival of planet Earth, and continue to slaughter each other in vast numbers – a trait without parallel in the animal world.

Part of the reason for our incredible technical advance from making fire and brewing beer to space travel and cybernetics is that human beings are intrinsically inventive and innovative. That can be seen in the exploratory and experimental learning of very young children. And yet the planet is ridden with conflict to such an extent that the 2011 Global Monitoring Report (GMR) on progress towards the goal of Education for All (EFA) has had to be focused on human conflict and education. Seeds of conflict and territorial control can also be seen in very young children, which gives us a clue as to why Illich was concerned about the recognition of informal education, which resides in the culture of families and communities and is a lifelong process and experience for us all. Schooling is also culturally embedded, but rather in the context of the evolution of the wider society where two main indicators of culture, language and religion, have played their part. It is politically controlled and delivered in a formalized way, which is why it is part of formal education. Operating on a different scale as a legal requirement, it can easily be in conflict with informal education. On top of all that we learn from our engagement with civil society, through our occupation, through our membership of organizations (which may include the religious), through recreational activities and so on, all of which constitute non-formal education.

Where we are at with education almost everywhere is a situation of disconnect between its three forms, which fails to take account of our essential humanity and limits our capacity to resolve biological, societal, economic and environmental problems we have created at all levels of scale from the global to the local. Human beings are not only technically innovative and dangerously competitive. They can also be imaginative and creative – qualities that are not often employed at a policy level, though they need to be. We are going to have to overcome convention and inertia if education is no longer to be a global concern.

# Abbreviations

| | |
|---|---|
| APC | African, Pacific and Caribbean |
| BRAC | Bangladesh Rural Advancement Committee |
| CAR | Central African Republic |
| CXC | Caribbean Examinations Council |
| DfID | Department for International Development |
| DG | Directorate General (of the European Commission) |
| DRC | Democratic Republic of Congo |
| EFA | Education for All |
| EHEA | European Higher Education Area |
| EHR | Education as a Humanitarian Response |
| EU | European Union |
| FAO | Food and Agriculture Organization |
| GATS | General Agreement on Trade and Services |
| GBO-3 | Third Global Biodiversity Outlook |
| GMR | Global Monitoring Reports |
| HEI | Higher Education Institution |
| IBE | International Bureau of Education |
| ICT | Information and Communications Technology |
| IDP | Internally Displaced People |
| ILO | International Labour Organization |
| IMF | International Monetary Fund |
| INEE | Inter-Agency Network for Education in Emergencies |
| LEA | Local Education Authority |
| MDG | Millennium Development Goal |
| MENA | Middle Eastern and North African |
| MSF | Médecins Sans Frontières |
| NAFTA | North American Free Trade Agreement |
| NGO | Non-Governmental Organization |
| OECD | Organisation for Economic Co-operation and Development |

| | |
|---|---|
| OJT | On-the-Job-Training |
| OVCs | Orphans and Vulnerable Children |
| PAR | Participatory Action Research |
| PISA | Programme for International Student Assessment |
| PRC | People's Republic of China |
| PROCAM | Promotion and Capacity-building in the Amazon |
| SGBV | Sexual and Gender Based Violence |
| TB | Tuberculosis |
| TESSA | Teacher Education in sub-Saharan Africa |
| TIMMS | Trends in International Maths and Science Study |
| UNDP | United Nations Development Programme |
| UNESCO | United Nations Educational, Scientific and Cultural Organization |
| UNHCR | United Nations High Commissioner for Refugees |
| UNICEF | United Nations Children's Emergency Fund |
| UNIFEM | United Nations Development Fund for Women |
| UNRWA | United Nations Relief and Works Agency |
| UNU | United Nations University |
| UPE | Universal Primary Education |
| WHO | World Health Organization |
| WISE | Wilberforce Institute for the study of Slavery and Emancipation |
| WTO | World Trade Organization |
| WUS | World University Service |

# Why is Education a Global Concern?

## Introduction

Education in the sense that most people conceive of it has a great deal to answer for. It has massive potential for good in terms of maximizing the capacity of human populations to relate positively to each other in the interest of mutual well-being. It also has massive potential for informing human populations about the state of planet Earth and how to respect its various environments and natural resources in the interests of sustainable development. It has failed on both counts, as David Orr observed nearly twenty years ago:

> It is time I believe for an educational 'perestroika', by which I mean a general rethinking of the process and substance of education at all levels, beginning with the admission that much of what has gone wrong with the world is the result of education that alienates us from life in the name of human domination, fragments instead of unifies, overemphasises success and careers, separates feeling from intellect and the practical from the theoretical and unleashes on the world

minds ignorant of their own ignorance. As a result, an increasing percentage of human intelligence must attempt to undo a large part of what mere intellectual cleverness has done carelessly and greedily.

(Orr, 1994, 17)

David Orr's distinction between 'human intelligence' and 'intellectual cleverness' is fundamental to understanding why education is a concern at all scales from global to local. The priorities that have come to dominate formal schooling, and the assessment of achievement within it, lean more towards the intellectual cleverness end of the spectrum of learning. They also give priority to technical and instrumental skills, so that success in acquiring these skills has come to dominate the curriculum and what most people expect from schools. But schools are part of society and need to relate more to the contexts in which they operate if those skills are to be used intelligently in the future by the young adults that emerge from the formal process. Concern as to whether this is happening can be illustrated by two examples from the media.

In November 2009, the *Guardian* published two significant items indicating concern about education. The first was an article by a former minister of education, Estelle Morris, under the title 'A Legal Right to a Good Education Doesn't Mean that You'll Get One'. This was an informed observation on the school system in England, one of the most developed countries in the world – a system a significant proportion of whose products fail to reach minimum standards of literacy, numeracy and basic life skills required to access meaningful employment. Referring to the meeting of minimum standards, she continued:

> If a school system is to deliver these new guarantees, it must get three things right in every single school. First, and most important, there must be effective teaching and visionary leadership; second, every child needs the social capital that will give them the resilience to be successful learners, and third, parents must deliver on their responsibility to make sure children arrive at school ready to learn.
>
> (Morris, 2009)

It is clear that the first requirement, though necessary, has no chance of being delivered without the cooperation of the second and the third. For a significant proportion of the world's population the basic challenges they face merely to survive make such conditions extremely difficult to meet, to say the least. They need assistance, whether indirect in the form of a fairer global economic system, or direct in the form of specific aid, and not just educational aid. Such assistance is normally regarded as being of a 'humanitarian nature', often in response to a disaster either natural or man-made. But is a concept as fundamental as 'humanitarian' relevant in educational terms only to those who are marginalized or excluded from mainstream education systems?

The second example, also from the *Guardian* of November 2009, was a four-page 'Advertisement Promotion' and free DVD under the very meaningful title: 'We Are the People We've Been Waiting For'. Both the advertisement narrative and the DVD follow the experiences of five teenagers from a typical English town, whose education and employment prospects have been rescued by significant involvement in forms of and opportunities for learning outside the compulsory school environment. That is to say, they have enhanced their social capital, and in four of the five cases enjoyed the parental support to which Estelle Morris referred. In the fifth case that support was provided by the child-care system. It is worthy of note that the contributors to the DVD were not professional educators but high achievers in creative fields such as writing, film-making and self-made wealth creation.

The key message carried by both these contributions to the education debate is that schools cannot function effectively unless they are in tune with civil society, which is itself informed by non-formal and informal education. So the first step in addressing the feeling that education is a global concern is to ask the question, 'What is "education" anyway?'

## What is 'education' anyway?

It is unlikely that we will find a definition from the education establishment that would satisfy the critics whose concerns are outlined above. As we shall see below, that establishment is part of the problem. More illuminating are the observations of two prominent figures from civil society, George Bernard Shaw and Bill Shankley. Shaw, the famous playwright and satirist, had it that 'schooling is an unfortunate interruption in the process of education', and there is more than a grain of truth in that observation, especially for those in compulsory state schooling systems. Shankley, who came from an impoverished mining community, left school young and went into professional soccer, eventually becoming the greatest manager of Liverpool Football Club. When asked to explain his success, he replied, 'I didn't have any education, therefore I had to use my brains,' a very perceptive response. Both recognize, albeit indirectly, the limited role that formal schooling plays in the education of an individual.

So, if schooling is not the same as education, what is education? It comprises the processes of learning and teaching that are ongoing throughout our lives, and evident in three forms: formal, non-formal and informal. Here are my definitions of the three forms of education:

LIVERPOOL JOHN MOORES UNIVERSITY
LEARNING SERVICES

- *Informal education* comprises the phenomena of teaching and learning as enabled by gratuitous or involuntary means.
- *Non-formal education* is the phenomenon of organized teaching and learning enabled by agencies or institutions that are not normally recognized as part of an official educational system, especially the so-called 'compulsory phase'.
- *Formal education* is the phenomenon of organized teaching and learning as enabled by the components of a recognized system of institutions such as schools, colleges and universities, and especially of the compulsory phase.

As with any classification or typology, these three categories of education are not mutually exclusive. They overlap, as illustrated in Figure 1.1.

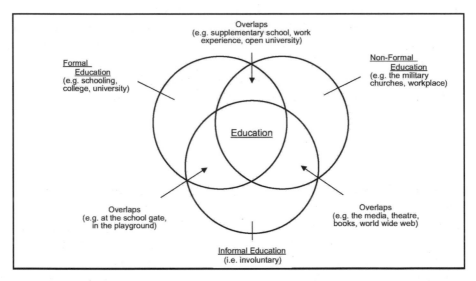

*Figure 1.1  Forms of Education*

The American historian of education, Lawrence Cremin (1988), came close to defining the totality of education as follows:

> As in the first two volumes I have defined education broadly, as the deliberate, systematic and sustained effort to transmit, evoke or acquire knowledge, values, attitudes, skills and sensibilities, as well as any learning that results from that effort, direct or indirect, intended or unintended.
>
> (Cremin, 1988)

It is clear that the vast majority of the world's population is experiencing a great deal of informal education, though this will be extremely limited in such contexts as severe deprivation, conflict or captivity. A significant proportion will be experiencing some form of non-formal education even if it does not come from an agency or institution. Likewise, most will be experiencing some degree of formal education, though for the majority of those it will be relatively brief and and/or dysfunctional. The dominance of the informal dimension simply reflects the fact that educational experience of all kinds is culturally embedded to a degree that varies considerably from place to place. That is to say it is extremely *locale specific*. Consequently, attempts by governments, or even more local political authorities, to impose policies throughout the area of their jurisdiction are often moderated, or even ignored, at the local level. For example, in England the institution of systems of school choice are often 'played' to their own advantage by neighbouring headteachers who do not wish merely to compete, as well as by the better-off parents who do. At the other end of the spectrum in the poorest countries, where the majority of the global population reside, local factors take over for a wide variety of reasons. In many cases the formal school systems are incomplete, especially in locations remote from official reach, funding and control. Many of the poorer nations of the world are extremely multicultural and multilingual, so that even if schooling provision is available, its nature and effect will vary enormously from one locality to another.

In any case, it is well known that mental capabilities and other talents for the acquisition of knowledge and skills are specific to the individual. We may require people to go to school, to follow particular curricula and to undertake examinations and other forms of assessment. But the outcome only tells us a small part of the story of their overall learning experience. The real curriculum, that is to say the totality of educational outcomes, formal, non-formal and informal for any individual, cannot be comprehended; not even by themselves. This has not prevented governments all over the world from constructing systems of formal education, and in almost every case requiring attendance for a defined period of time. What are these systems actually for, and why are they so similar across the globe?

# Education systems and their functions

Education systems are what we mean by formal education. Despite the extraordinary variety of cultures, languages and religions within the global population, these systems are remarkably similar. They are based on the combined legacy of Graeco-Roman culture and the traditions of the Abrahamic religions: Judaism, Christianity and Islam. All these were informed by older learning institutions to the east in what are now India and Pakistan, where the earliest universities were founded. The key characteristics of this 'European Model', derived from classical Greece and Rome but kept alive and developed by Arab scholarship in the so-called 'dark ages', were urban based, highly elitist and male dominated. From about the twelfth century AD onwards they became a crucial part of the means for the domination of territory by a combination of church and state, and were exported around the globe by European colonialism. Of course, there were already forms of organized learning elsewhere, such as the schools of Aztec Mexico and the imperial system of ancient China. However, the European model either simply replaced them as part of the conquest, as in Mexico, or was taken on board as part of late-nineteenth-century-modernization, as in China and Japan. At the community level, indigenous and highly localized educational practices continued, such as indigenous African education, but became challenged by the colonial model. In the metropoles, massification of this model occurred as European nation states became urbanized in association with industrialization. An illiterate workforce was no longer feasible as the economies of these nation states diversified, and both churches and governments were forced to accept wider access to schooling for practical reasons. With industrialization requiring mass literacy and numeracy, compulsory schooling developed, and ever since a direct relationship between formal education and national economic performance has been assumed, though never clarified.

Consequently, the functions of compulsory schooling are clear:

1  as social and political *control mechanisms* of the state;
2  in particular as mechanisms of *selection and allocation* of individuals to different life-paths and chances;
3  for the *acquisition of knowledge and skills* conventionally believed to enhance the national economy;
4  for the *custody of children and young people* in urban environments where, unlike their rural counterparts, they have nothing constructive to do when the adults are working.

It must, of course, be recognized that there were humanitarian elements involved as well, such as combating practices of child labour in factories and mines, and the provision of equal opportunities for girls. Nonetheless, the prime function of *selection* is evident in most education systems on the basis of the relative merits of diffuse and technical skills as well as social models ranging from aristocratic (by privilege), through meritocratic (by competition) to socialistic (by cooperation). In practice, additional factors such as social class, ethnicity and gender often play a significant part in patterns of selection.

Despite this range of issues, the structure of national education systems is virtually uniform throughout the world based on the mainly chronological stages primary, secondary and tertiary. We are so familiar with this that it is difficult to conceive of anything else, yet this sequence only covers an age range of about twenty years (about six to twenty-six) from kindergarten to PhD, and that for a tiny minority. For the majority, of course, the actual experience is for up to ten years, including the most rapidly changing and difficult period of young adolescence. For far too many of the world's population it is five years or fewer, if at all. Technical and vocational education may form an alternative secondary or tertiary pathway, but it is often afforded less regard and support. This makes the charts of national education systems so misleading as to be virtually pointless. Together with the at best partial, and at worst fraudulent, statistics fed into international databases they shed very little light on the realities and outcomes of educational experiences.

In addition to structural conformity, curriculum content is often ill-related to individual and local needs at any given time. Like structures, curricula are derived from developed urbanized countries either by colonial legacy or by more recent neo and post-colonial globalization. While the recognition of broad subject categories may be appropriate, the content often is not. In the poorer majority of the world's population, promotion to the next grade of schooling depends on passing the annual examination. The relevance of the subject matter to family and local needs comes into question, and parents may well withdraw their children from school. They cannot see what function the system is serving on behalf of their offspring, their family and their community. The opportunity cost is just too high.

# Education and development

As mentioned above, public education systems came into being in response to the perceived needs of the economies of European nation states and their colonial offshoots. They emerged with different degrees of centralization for political and ideological reasons. In the early British colonies of what later became the USA, control over schooling was highly localized due to the small-scale survival communities involved. Many of these became school districts, as individual colonies, such as Massachusetts, formalized their public provision. After independence the founding fathers of the nation wisely excluded the federal government from control over education in the Constitution of the USA. Instead, by default, they vested this responsibility in the hands of the individual states of the union as well as in school districts. By contrast, post-revolutionary and Napoleonic France established a highly centralized national system. Between these two extremes lay all kinds of arrangements. In England and Wales the neo-liberal laissez-faire approach of successive Victorian governments meant that nothing resembling a national state system emerged until 1902, and even then was very partial until at least 1944.

Both France and Britain applied their national philosophies of education to the colonies comprising their respective empires: the systems of so-called 'direct' and 'indirect' rule. After independence from their colonial masters virtually all the emerging nations invested heavily in public education, believing there to be a direct connection between such investment and economic development. In this they were deluded. There is a connection, of course, but it is indirect, extremely complex, and neither uniform nor yet understood. It is likely to be very different between nations, and indeed between their various regions and localities, as education is just one of many factors involved in social and economic development.

One such factor is geopolitics. Take, for example, Ukraine. As one of the key Republics of the USSR for seventy years, Ukraine benefited from the highly inclusive and non-selective polytechnical school system of the federation. This, together with its unique location within the USSR – relative proximity to Moscow, containing the highly productive 'bread-basket' of the steppelands, and possessing the only significant warm-water coastline for the Soviet fleet – made Ukraine a favoured area economically. Since 1990 it has been an independent country no longer supported by Russia, but still subject to its powerful proximity, and for the foreseeable future unlikely to be able to join the European Union. Educational standards remain extremely high because, as elsewhere, they depend on cultural tradition, but their ability to enhance development has been considerably weakened. This is not, of course, to say that Ukrainians do not value their freedom, but rather that the scope for high educational standards to contribute to development has been severely constrained by geopolitical change.

Presumably because of the assumed but unproven and therefore naive belief in an automatic connection between investment in public education systems and economic growth, international development agencies, especially the World Bank, invested heavily in economists. For some forty years after the foundation of such agencies, this investment may have been more of a hindrance than a help. Competing theories battled for influence on development aid policy culminating in the disastrous implementation of structural adjustment, an approach only really manageable in more developed economies such as that of Britain in the 1980s. Then around 1990 research began to indicate that, in the developing world at least, investment in the education of individuals at a basic level, such as primary schooling and adult literacy, enabled development by aggregation rather than in the mass. This comes back to the point made earlier that the efficacy of educational experience is highly individual and idiosyncratic. Identifying the talents of the individual, and fostering them through formal schooling, had been advocated centuries ago by Jean-Jacques Rousseau, but the advent of national systems of education with their rigid curricula could not accommodate them. More recently, Howard Gardner at Harvard in the 1980s put forward his theory of 'multiple intelligences', advocating the recognition of the unique set of talents of individuals and the need to foster them for the personal and collective good. Unfortunately this too has been largely sidelined.

# The Millennium Development Goals

The onset of the millennium in 2000 coincided with a ten-year review at Dakar, Senegal, of the outcome of the 1990 global education conference at Jomtien in Thailand. This had picked up on development by aggregation, and strongly recommended focusing investment on primary/basic schooling rather than secondary and higher education. This ten-year millennium review is known as the Dakar Accord, and reinforced the focus on primary/basic schooling for national development. It led in turn to the formulation of the 'Millennium Development Goals' (MDGs), eight in number of which only one, MDG 2, had to do directly with education, but of which all the others have clear implications for education. Table 1.1 details the targets of the MDGs.

The direct and explicit focus on achieving universal primary education (UPE), together with achieving gender parity in schooling, reinforced the focus of development aid to education on the primary/basic sector. This seemed to sideline the fact that research and teaching in higher education institutions (HEIs) would be vital to meeting the challenges of all the MDGs. UNESCO and the World Bank had already begun to show concern about this with a joint taskforce, which reported in Paris in 1998 on advocating partnerships between HEIs and other sectors of education, formal and non-formal. This may well have informed the nature of MDG 8, but in any case UNESCO followed up with a series of Higher Education Forums through the early 2000s.

| Goal | Summary of targets (T) |
| --- | --- |
| 1 Eradicate Extreme Poverty and Hunger | T1: Considerably reduce % of people on $US1 per day.<br>T2: full productive work for all.<br>T3: Considerably reduce % of people who suffer hunger. |
| 2 Achieve UPE | T1: completion of full primary course for all by 2015. |
| 3 Gender Equality | T1: Achieve at primary and secondary by 2005 and all levels 2015. |
| 4 Reduce Child Mortality | T1: Considerably reduce the child mortality rate by 2015. |
| 5 Improve Maternal Health | T1: Reduce maternal mortality ratio by 75%.<br>T2: Achieve universal access to reproductive health. |
| 6 Combat HIV/AIDS, Malaria and Other Diseases | T1: Reduce by 50% and begin to reverse HIV/AIDS.<br>T2: Universal access to treatment for HIV/AIDS by 2010 for all who need it.<br>T3: By 2015 to halt and begin to reverse the influence of malaria and other major diseases. |
| 7 Ensure Environmental Sustainability | T1: Get sustainable development into natural policies and conserve environmental resources.<br>T2: Reduce biodiversity loss considerably by 2010.<br>T3: Reduce by 50 percent the proportion of people with no sustainable access to safe drinking water and sanitation.<br>T4: To achieve by 2020 a significant improvement in the lives of at least 100 million slum dwellers. |
| 8 Develop a Global Partnership for Development | T1: Address the special needs of the least developed countries, landlocked countries and small island developing states.<br>T2: Develop an open, rule-based, predictable non-discriminatory trading and financial system.<br>T3: Deal comprehensively with developing countries' debt.<br>T4: Work with pharmaceutical companies to provide access to affordable essential drugs in developing countries. |

*Table 1.1  A Summary of the Millennium Development Goals (MDGs)*

Nonetheless, the focus of education for development remained on the primary/basic sector under the title of Education for All (EFA). In order to track progress towards EFA, a unit was established, housed at UNESCO headquarters in Paris, to monitor and report on progress towards EFA. At the time of writing it has produced eight EFA Global

Monitoring Reports (GMRs). These are not limited to UPE, though strongly focused on it. Some have a specific issue, as can be seen from the list of GMRs up to 2010 in Table 1.2.

| Date | Theme |
|------|-------|
| 2002 | *Education for All: Is the World on Track?* |
| 2003/4 | *Gender and Education for All: The Leap to Equality* |
| 2005 | *Education for Al: The Quality Imperative* |
| 2006 | *Literacy for Life* |
| 2007 | *Strong Foundations: Early Childhood Care and Education* |
| 2008 | *Education for All by 2015: Will We Make It?* |
| 2009 | *Overcoming Inequality: Why Governance Matters* |
| 2010 | *Reaching the Marginalized* |

*Table 1.2 EFA Global Monitoring Reports 2002–10*

The inclusion of the acronym EFA in the collective identity of the GMRs implies a focus on basic schooling despite the broader themes in the titles of some of them. While all the themes to date are clearly important, it is perhaps surprising that there has yet to be a GMR with a strong focus on teachers or on technical/vocational education or adult education. Teacher supply and quality is one of three most important issues for the effectiveness of schooling as implied in the quotation from Estelle Morris at the beginning of this chapter, especially the enhancement of skills to identify and foster the individual talents of the young. Another is family, and especially parental support. That in every country enabling the potential of children and young people to be realized depends considerably on the educational level of adults in the family and community should be self-evident. Teachers in school are just one category of adult involved.

As the sequence of GMRs has developed there has been some progress from an initial tendency to view the objectives and evaluation of EFA in terms of rates of enrolment, completion and attainment and a focus on mainstream primary schooling. Consequently, in the eighth GMR, *Reaching the Marginalized* (2010c), five EFA goals and progress towards them are discussed in detail:

1    Early childhood care and education
2    Universal primary education (includes gender parity)

3  Youth and adult skills
4  Adult literacy
5  The quality of education

It then proceeds to evaluate overall progress in terms of 'The Education for All Development Index', taking into account all these goals, but the prime role of formal schooling is evident in the following summary of 'quality':

> Millions of children are emerging from school each year without having acquired basic literacy and numeracy skills. Policy-makers, educators and parents need to focus more on the core purpose of education, ensuring that children acquire the skills that shape their future life chances.

It would seem that a focus on the connection between formal schooling and national development, a relationship that is assumed to be direct but is little understood and certainly unproven, could well be a cause for concern. The assumption goes little beyond a simple correlation that juxtaposes education and GNP. Britain was at its most wealthy and powerful vis-à-vis other nations in the late nineteenth century when universal primary education had not yet been achieved, and there was almost no access to secondary schooling for the vast majority. Colonialism and exploitation governed and managed by a privileged elite was the engine of national wealth and power. Over a hundred years later, such a means of wealth creation has long since ceased to be acceptable, though it is attempted here and there. Clearly there is no simple explanation for the correlation between formal education provision and national economic success where it exists. But as A.C. Grayling (2001) observes:

> Education, and especially 'liberal education' is what makes civil society possible. That means it has an importance even greater than its contribution to economic success, which, alas, is all that politicians seem to think it is for.
>
> (Grayling, 2001, 157)

Politicians govern national education systems and are the paymasters. They are part of an 'education establishment', and that is the next reason why education is a global concern.

# The problem of the education establishment

It is not only governments and international organizations of the kind that have created the MDGs and GMRs which tend to take a very narrow view of education by concentrating on the formal dimension. There is the problem of the education establishment as well. This comprises civil servants in ministries of education, education inspectors and administrators at other levels (including head teachers), and academics in departments of educational studies in universities and colleges.

The civil servants and administrators may be expected to operate merely as functionaries of government, whether national or sub-national (as in the states of the USA, the Länder of Germany or the provinces of China), but in practice they have a great deal of influence on decision-making and control. Their concentration is on formal education and enabling the operation of the two main functions of national school systems outlined above: social control and the delivery of a certain limited range of knowledge and skills deemed to be conducive to economic development. Teachers, at least in the public sector of schooling, have to operate within this framework. Academics, that is to say educationists, might be expected to adopt a more critical and radical stance, but few do. To be fair, a significant proportion of them are teacher trainers and so must concentrate on that task, which relates directly to schooling. They may be able to be radical and innovate in a technical and instrumental sense, but only within the curriculum confines laid down by governments. If opportunity for reflection occurs it tends to be in relation to self-assessment of performance in the classroom or other management-related issues.

Research is a distinctive function of academics, and at university level must be of a critical and an analytical nature to be credible. This is something that governments, whether national or sub-national, tend to be very uneasy about and control as much as possible. One way to do this is to control as much of the funding of research as possible, and ascribe higher status to studies supported by their own research agencies. This can affect the potential status of academics through promotion, as research output is the main criterion involved. If academics gain funding from independent sources such as charitable trusts and their findings are critical of the system, or any part of it, then governments may simply disregard them or even discredit them unfairly. An example of this is the University of Cambridge research project on primary schooling in England known as the Cambridge Primary Review (Alexander, 2009), funded by the Esmee Fairbairn Foundation and published in 2009. An exemplary project headed by the leading expert on the subject in the UK, it was consigned to the waste-bin by the government immediately on publication. A decade earlier, a senior government functionary commissioned a young academic to conduct a review of educational research in England with a view to discrediting it. As it turned out, the methods of this research mercenary turned out to be as flawed as he painted the researches of his peers to be. Such examples are by no means confined to Britain as most governments are determined to keep control of what is taught in schools and how. Politicians base their policies on education on factors that are little related to the real issues and concerns. One reason is that they have their own ideological convictions about schooling, which is the only education sector that directly affects the majority of voters. Another is that if a politician gains high office as, say, minister of education, their period in power may well be short – often two or three years at most. Educational processes, reforms and outcomes for the individuals involved operate on a time scale of, for most, at least ten years.

When education as a discipline developed in nineteenth-century Europe and especially the USA, its nature as an interdisciplinary field was recognized through the contribution of a range of fields. For while all subjects are disciplines, not all disciplines are subjects. Education, or educational studies, is not a subject, but a composite discipline, as illustrated in Figure 1.2. It relies on the application and contribution of other fields, some of them contributing disciplines as well, such as geography, history and economics.

With the contraction of educational studies into an instrumental mode, little space is left for the educational foundations as they are known, such as history of education, sociology of education, economics of education, comparative education, philosophy of education and even psychology of education. The geography of education has hardly developed, which is a curious omission give that educational practices and land use are just as susceptible to locational and spatial analysis as, for example, health care or manufacturing industry. Sadly, nowadays very little research in the educational foundations penetrates beyond their dwindling tribal memberships.

In any case, most academics in educational studies are not operating in these fields. Research is driven by its funding sources, primarily governments, who are concerned above all with performance, attainment and 'value for money' in the formal state system. As mentioned above, academic careers are evaluated entirely on research output. In the UK, for example, the Research Assessment Exercise, in operation for two decades, has introduced an invidious pecking order of funding sources.

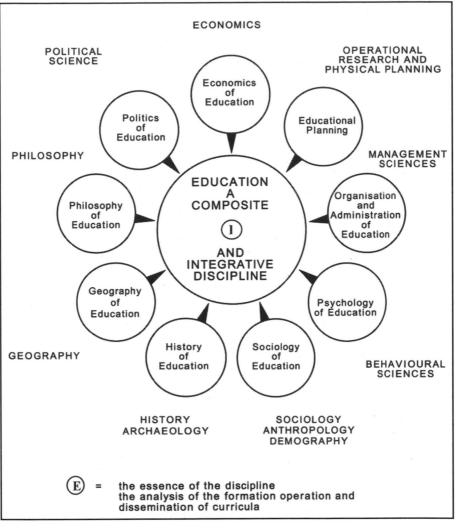

ECONOMICS

POLITICAL
SCIENCE

OPERATIONAL
RESEARCH AND
PHYSICAL PLANNING

Economics
of
Education

Politics
of
Education

Educational
Planning

PHILOSOPHY

MANAGEMENT
SCIENCES

EDUCATION
A
COMPOSITE

Philosophy
of
Education

Organisation
and
Administration
of
Education

Ⓘ

AND
INTEGRATIVE
DISCIPLINE

Geography
of
Education

Psychology
of Education

GEOGRAPHY

History
of
Education

Sociology
of
Education

BEHAVIOURAL
SCIENCES

HISTORY
ARCHAEOLOGY

SOCIOLOGY
ANTHROPOLOGY
DEMOGRAPHY

Ⓔ = the essence of the discipline
the analysis of the formation operation and
dissemination of curricula

*Figure 1.2   Education: a composite and integrative discipline*

The same has been done for the publications in which the outcomes and discussions appear. Most academics in this and other fields will understandably play the system to the advantage of themselves and the departments and institutions to which they belong, but in so doing they become part of the establishment.

Political power over education has long been the preserve of governments. For example, in 1805 in England, Leeds Grammar School was taken to task for wishing to introduce modern languages into the curriculum. There was no minister of education at that time, indeed not for over a further hundred years, but the Lord Chancellor of the day ruled the innovation to be against the terms of the school's endowment, interpreted to be to provide a 'classical education'. This also affected science. Two hundred years later in England and the USA, policies of diversification in schooling provision, encouraged or supported by provincial or national governments, have enabled creationists in positions of power to deny the findings of credible scientists in the school curriculum. Control over the school curriculum can become a battleground, and this has been enhanced by international surveys of attainment in a limited number of subjects. Beginning decades ago in the form of the International Evaluation of Achievement (IEA) surveys, which ranged across a large number of subjects in the school curriculum, there has been a trend in recent times to narrow the focus. The Trends in International Maths and Science Study (TIMMS) is a case in point, having been undertaken in 1995, 1999, 2003 and 2007, and due again in 2011. In concentrating only on these two areas of the school curriculum, it implies a significance for these greater than that afforded to other subjects in relation to a nebulous connection with national well-being, especially economic. But TIMMS refers only to grades 4 and 8 in the school succession. Overall in 2007, involving forty-five nations, it represented just over a quarter of the nations of the world at eighth grade as follows: Africa 5 (3 in North Africa); Asia 21 (not including China and India); Europe 16; North America 2 (not including Canada); South America 1 (not Brazil); and Oceania 1 (Australia). So here we have an ongoing legacy embedded in the global consciousness of governments, which is extremely partial educationally as well as in terms of participation, with China, Brazil and India not yet represented at eighth grade.

The legitimacy of information provided by some participating nations has been challenged, as have criteria and methods of international comparison (Postlethwaite, 1999). Nonetheless, governments continue to participate – even more so in the Programme for International Student Assessment (PISA). PISA has the credibility of having been developed and operated by the prestigious Organisation for Economic Co-operation and Development (OECD), founded in 1961 and based in Paris. Membership is based on having reached a relatively high level of national economic development, and currently includes some thirty countries. Of these twenty-three are in Europe, three in North America (NAFTA), plus Australia, Japan, South Korea and New Zealand. The PISA programme has, to date, operated four times – in 2000, 2003, 2006 and 2009 – and from the outset has been open to some non-member countries participating. Consequently there were 43 participants in 2000, 41 in 2003, 57 in 2006 and 65 in 2009. It is based on standardized tests being administered to a selection of fifteen-year-olds in 2009. These were in four areas of the curriculum: reading literacy, mathematics literacy, science literacy and problem solving. According to the PISA website in January 2010, its:

> Economic modelling relates cognitive skills – as measured by PISA and other international instruments to economic growth, demonstrating that relatively small improvements to labour force skills can largely impact the future well-being of a nation.

OECD itself indicates that 'complex methodologies are used to collect and process the data', but since only a selection of fifteen-year-olds are involved, it must be presumed that only the formal schooling they have received in a limited range of the curriculum is deemed to be responsible for development and the prediction of national well-being in decades to come. Does this mean that labour force skills are not enhanced by anything else, such as the non-formal education and training provided by employers? Does this mean that other components of school curricula make no contribution?

These are matters of concern because when things go wrong, schools and teachers are blamed by governments, as they were, for example, when the USSR beat the USA to become the first nation to put a satellite into orbit around the earth (Sputnik, 1957) and then the first man into space (Yuri Gagarin, 1961). American high schools received massive criticism at the time, much as schools in Britain did for the loss of the Boer War in South Africa in 1902, and as French schools did in respect of the debacle that was the Franco-Prussian War of 1870–71.

So while it is self-evident that effective schooling is more likely to make a positive contribution to the human capital of individuals than poor schooling, it must also be the case that, as per A.C. Grayling's observation quoted above, it is a pity that this is all that politicians think formal education is for.

## Summary

So why is education a global concern? This discussion has attempted to outline a number of reasons, of which the first and perhaps most important is the tendency to equate formal education, and especially schooling, with 'education'. In reality, it is only one part of the education of any individual, assuming they can get it. Such a view seriously detracts from the greater influence of informal and non-formal education on providing the social capital and support systems that make effective learning and teaching possible. This is true in schooling as well as beyond and outside in the worlds of family, community and gainful employment.

Despite the undeniable importance and contribution of effective schooling, its direct contribution to individual well-being is compromised by the two main functions required of it by the state: namely, its role as part of the social and political control system and its role as the assumed prime contributor to national economic development. This is even evident in the strong focus on primary schooling in the EFA contribution to development as monitored by the annual GMRs, and in the strong focus on secondary schooling in a few subjects by TIMMS and PISA. In these two prestigious surveys the situation of the leading up-and-coming countries in the global economy – Brazil, China and India – is minimal or missing. It is telling that in 2009 China submitted a return to PISA only from Shanghai, its economic powerhouse. Education, seen in terms of formal schooling, has become highly politicized and reduced to positioning in league tables whether locally, regionally, nationally or internationally. Critical thinking in terms of disinterested educational research has been largely sidelined by policy-makers.

So there are many ways in which education in the formal sense is a cause for global concern. They range from having too much of it that is dysfunctional to not having access to any of it at all; from a focus on mass conformity and national targets to a lack of concern for the nurturing of individual talents. What is needed is a fresh look at the phenomenon of education, one that recognizes that the three forms of education are intricately interrelated and are responsive to individual circumstances, talents and needs. That fresh look can be served by seeing education as a humanitarian response.

# Education as a Humanitarian Response 2

## Introduction

It is a well-established conventional wisdom in education that if we get it right for the disadvantaged and those with special needs, we will likely get it right for the majority mainstream. Education as a humanitarian response (EHR) should be for everyone, at any particular time, place or circumstance, and appropriate to their individual needs as well as those of their families and local communities. At present, this is not the case in most places, and that is why, as indicated above, education is a global concern. In December 2008, the United Nations General Assembly inaugurated a World Humanitarian Day, with the aim of raising the profile of humanitarian assistance throughout the world. This of course included educational assistance, but the implication was that a humanitarian approach was specifically to do with the excluded, marginalized and disadvantaged. It is quite possible, and indeed often the case, that those with access to the mainstream of formal education can be marginalized or otherwise disadvantaged. Consequently, the concept of education as a humanitarian response being promoted here is holistic in nature.

# A holistic approach to EHR

What is being advocated here is, at the very least, recognizing education as a humanitarian response alongside the functions of national systems of education that already obtain: as control mechanisms maintaining and sustaining the status quo, and selection mechanisms for servicing the economy and economic development. Those functions are for the collective whereas EHR looks to an approach that is for the individual, locale-specific, and necessarily relating closely to specific needs and cultures at any particular time and place. Such an approach would require a considerable degree of freedom from the state, though not necessarily total freedom. It implies a willingness to trust professional educators at all levels. This is rarely the case now: they are reduced to mere functionaries – teachers teaching to the test, or researchers shackled by the system. Figure 2.1 seeks to illustrate a holistic approach.

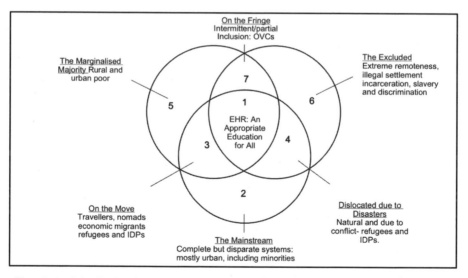

*Fig. 2.1  A holistic view of education as a humanitarian response*

Figure 2.1 is, of course, not to scale, as a majority of the world's population is being, will be or has already been subjected to the mainstream experience to some degree. Neither is it a systems diagram. Nonetheless, it indicates that EHR is an ideal condition when all three categories, the included, the marginalized and the excluded, overlap. The following paragraphs further illustrate this by addressing each of the segments of Figure 2.1, from 1 through 7.

1 *Full inclusion* within a provision that *functions appropriately* in meeting the educational needs of all in a situation of sustainable social and economic development, where informal and non-formal education are enabled to contribute effectively to generating social capital for civil society. Given the nature and functions of national systems of formal education, this optimum situation may well not exist anywhere in the world as yet. The most likely candidates to have achieved such harmony would be small isolated self-sufficient communities out of the reach of such national systems, but for other reasons they would also qualify for category 7. However, these qualities existed in most indigenous traditional forms of education prior to the impact of colonialism as discussed in Part 1 of Brown and Hiskett (1975). With respect to indigenous African education prior to European and Arab incursions, they say:

> Schooling, in the sense of institutionalised induction into the life of society is a comparatively recent development in Africa; education in the sense of initiation into the life of the adult community is a very ancient concept. In many parts of Africa this initiation has owed nothing to the influence of the world religions of Christianity and Islam. In this section, the authors show how this ancient concept is still very much part of the complicated overall provision of education in Africa.
>
> (Brown and Hiskett, 1975, 19)

2 *Full inclusion* in a mainstream system that is *dysfunctional* in that it fails to provide appropriately for the needs of all groups, and is selective by overt or covert means to the detriment of the chances of a greater or lesser proportion of the population, as well as to the potential contributions of non-formal and informal education. This is the case in complete mainstream systems of all countries sufficiently well developed to be able to afford and operate them. It obtains whether the national population is near homogeneous, as in China, or highly multicultural and multilingual, as in India. Formal education systems are politically driven and provided. They are then moderated by cultural and pragmatic issues on the ground. It is a matter of scale. Even in countries where a federal arrangement exists, as in Nigeria or Brazil, each state or province is still comparatively large to be dealing with the numerous small-scale variations within. Structural and regulatory variations might exist between localities, as was the case before the mid-1960s in England when the chances of 'passing' the Eleven Plus selective

examination for entry to a grammar school varied considerably according to how many such schools existed in any one locality. More recently in England the so-called postcode lottery and demographic changes have made equitable school choice policies inoperable. There are innumerable other disparities. Take, for example, children and young people in official care. In Britain, despite normal access to mainstream schooling, the majority of such people achieve much lower levels of attainment than any other group. These and other factors leading to high and multiple levels of disparity in educational chances mean that education as a humanitarian response is a necessary new objective everywhere.

3   *Minority groups* such as racial, ethnic, religious and linguistic groups, travellers, refugees, asylum seekers and economic migrants may be accommodated in the mainstream, but their particular needs are often not met to any significant degree. There are sometimes minority groups who outperform the mainstream average, such as those from the Lau island group in the Fijian archipelago. But in general, minority groups face special problems in national state education systems that fail to take into account their special cultural needs. They may be required to undertake schooling in a language not used or required in their particular family, location and economy, such as with the Harakambut in the Peruvian Amazon. Or they may simply be neglected, as is the case with the minorities such as the Garifuna in the so-called 'Atlantic' coastlands of Nicaragua; or persecuted like the settled Roma in a number of European countries. It could even be the case that a significant majority group is not receiving appropriate equitable attention. For example, a 2007 Joseph Rowntree Charitable Trust report in England focused on the underachievement of white-majority male school pupils. For some considerable time this group has, on average, achieved less well than white-majority girls and most ethnic minority pupils of both genders. This implies a lack of appropriate response on the part of the national system as well as the individuals themselves and their families. In extreme circumstances, a majority ethnic group may be segregated and thereby deliberately disadvantaged by the state, as in the former Apartheid system of the Republic of South Africa.

4   *Temporary exclusion* from the normal mainstream because of *disasters* due to: (a) *human causation* such as invasion/bombing, civil war, forced migration or internal displacement; (b) *natural events* such as earthquakes, tsunamis, floods, mudslides,

droughts or bushfires; (c) a *combination* of human and natural factors such as desertification due to overpopulation, overgrazing and large-scale conflict. Disasters of human causation are unfortunately numerous and growing in the twenty-first-century world. Examples include: the indiscriminate bombing of Gaza in 2008/9, which inevitably resulted in the destruction of Palestinian schools; the Iraq invasion of Kuwait which triggered the Gulf War in 1990/1; the civil war in Sierra Leone from 1991 to 2002; and forced migration and internal displacement in Iraq, Sudan and Colombia. Natural disasters inevitably affect education, with recent instances of earthquakes in Italy, China and Haiti; tsunamis in India, Sri Lanka and Indonesia; floods in China, the USA, UK and Poland; mudslides in Brazil and the Philippines; drought in Ethiopia; and bushfires in Australia. Examples of a combination of human and natural factors include Eritrea and Somalia in the Horn of Africa, where ongoing conflict has contributed to desertification, and Amazonian Brazil, where deforestation has degenerated the ecosystem and contributed to conflict and displacement. Responding to the educational needs of human groups in all of these circumstances has become known in recent times as *education in emergencies*.

5   *Marginalized communities* existing on the very fringes of the reach of the normal mainstream provision, usually due to remoteness, such as in desert environments in the Sindh Province of Pakistan, or the outer islands of an archipelago nation as in Vanuatu, the Philippines or Indonesia. In such places the education systems are incomplete, possibly only with primary schooling for some. Secondary provision, even if in theory a possibility through boarding, is ruled out for most by poverty and an unwillingness on the part of parents to put their children at potential risk. Genuine travelling communities, such as some Roma in Europe, the reindeer herders of the Arctic fringes and the Rabaris in the Ran of Kutch in India, come into this category.

6   *Excluded from mainstream provision.* This would include all who are excluded in practice for any reason. They may be explicitly excluded for reasons of culture, perhaps for being of the lowest social caste, like some Dalits in India. A very significant number of people in this category are those who live in illegal settlements, mainly the 'shanty towns' within or adjacent to major cities in some developing countries, such as in Manila, Mumbai, Nairobi and Sao Paulo. Some refugees fall into this category if they are in countries where they are forbidden access to the mainstream

of the host country, as are the Palestinians in refugee camps in Lebanon and the Karen people in refugee camps in Thailand. In these cases, however, they may be able to access their own forms of schooling within the camps provided by international agencies, NGOs or their own initiative. Also included in this category would be those in prison, though here too some special provision might be available by distance learning, for example in the case of adult offenders in Britain, through the Open University. Finally, there are those in slavery, whose numbers are considerable in various parts of the world. In some countries, for example Mauritania, what one might term basic, traditional forms of slavery exist, but this category ranges also across the large numbers, especially women and children, trafficked for sex and criminal purposes, and innumerable illegal immigrants in developed countries trapped by unscrupulous employers on minimal wages for fear of exposure and deportation.

7   *Wavering between marginalization and exclusion.* The most numerous and highly significant group in this category are orphans and vulnerable children (OVCs). They exist in all countries of the world, though their greater visibility in poorer countries, and especially urban locations, tends to categorize them merely as 'street children'. Some might be intermittently, or even regularly connected with elements of mainstream provision. For example in England, the Children's Society, an Anglican NGO, has operated projects in major cities to assist such children to re-engage with mainstream society, including schooling. Their work alone highlights the fact that so-called 'runaways' number in several hundreds at least in every city in the UK. In some parts of India, through a range of philanthropic and faith-based organizations, public and private schools assist the education of such children in various ways. An important group within the OVC category are 'working children', many of whom are not orphans but required to work by their parents, and may access schooling irregularly. In many developing countries these would be rural children, and especially girls. So the predominantly urban image of children on the margins of schooling is somewhat misleading. Of course, in many countries irregular attendance may lead to official exclusion, whether it be for truancy, health-related issues such as malnutrition or as a result of parental decision.

# A human rights approach

Another way of looking at this is from a human rights perspective, as exemplified in the following statement by UNHCR (the United Nations High Commissioner for Refugees, 2006), now known as the UN Refugee Agency:

> A new vision of quality education is essential and current events around the world have demonstrated that quality is not only about literacy and numeracy. There is a growing consensus that quality education cannot be limited to increasing the material inputs into the school systems or enhancing school effectiveness, important as they are. Quality education has both to be based on a human rights approach, and to address new areas including, but not limited to, cultural diversity, multilingualism in education, peace and non-violence, sustainable development and life skills.
>
> (UNHCR, 2006a)

This statement, though not in as many words, calls for education as a humanitarian response, and although it emanates from a source dealing with one of the most disadvantaged of human groups, does so in terms that apply equally well to all people and all forms of education. If the educational experience of any individual at any time or place is not appropriate, then neither is it humane. What is appropriate may well be difficult to determine but what is inhumane is easier to assess. If due regard is not given to the 'new areas' in the above quotation then there is no way in which education can be effective, and those new areas go well beyond the current focus on certain competencies supported by the influence of international tests and league tables engendered by TIMMS and PISA. Even the evaluations of the progress of EFA, which, as indicated in the previous chapter, are broadening in the right direction, are yet to address all these areas.

UNHCR, as an agency of the United Nations, is subject to some degree to the political pressures and procedures of its multinational parent. This includes the explicit policies of member governments and in particular those within whose territory it operates on behalf of the refugees therein. NGOs have also to be mindful of these constraints, but are by definition not politically constrained to the same degree. One of the leading NGOs operating in the field of education, especially but not exclusively in developing countries, is Save the Children UK. Alex Inglis (2007) summarized Save the Children's approach to 'quality education' as follows:

First the education a child receives must be relevant to their lifestyle, culture, location and future needs. It must be appropriate to the child's developmental progress, culture and language. In addition children must be fully active and participatory in their learning with families, and the wider community fully engaged in the process of learning of its children. Education must be flexible to differences between individual children, but at the same time respond effectively to the formal curriculum. Quality education is inherently linked to inclusive education which sees diversity of ability, gender and culture as a resource to support learning. Finally, education must be protective and safe from violence, abuse, conflict and exploitation.

(Inglis, 2007, 43)

The above quotations from UNHCR and, in respect of Save the Children from Inglis, clearly embrace the holistic imperative of education as a humanitarian response as well as a focus on the individual, the cultural context, the community, gender, flexibility, sustainable development and protection. They should apply globally.

## The issue of scale

It has been argued above that, irrespective of national regulations and their prime concern with the expected contribution of schooling to economic growth, what really happens in relation to education on the ground is much more complex and idiosyncratic than that. Complex in that informal and non-formal modes of education are prime movers rather than fringe players, and idiosyncratic in that context is crucial. There is also the imperative of flexibility in terms of response to need and to change. The centrality of context to a humanitarian response relates to the issue of spatial scale, while change has to do with temporal scale.

### Spatial scale

Spatial and locational issues are the concern of geography, and in this case the geography of education. As indicated above, both geography and educational studies are composite disciplines subject to a range of factors each informed by its own parent discipline. Figure 1.2 illustrated this in respect of education, while Figure 2.2 does the same for geography.

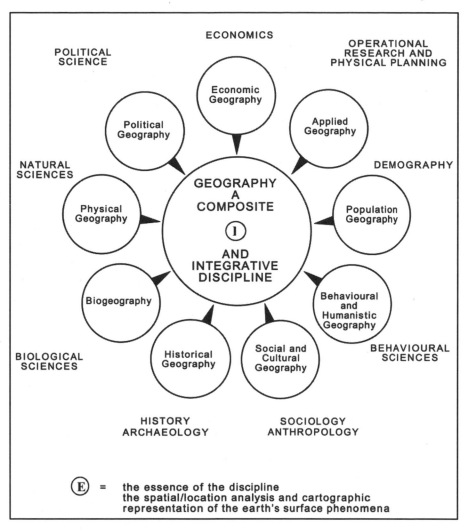

*Figure 2.2  Geography: a composite and integrative discipline*

We may apply this to any educational context. Take, for example, education in Sierra Leone, one of the world's poorest nations, emerging from a decade-long civil war. A clear grasp of the *historical geography* of education is necessary for the understanding of contemporary issues, which are always affected to some degree by the residual legacy of past educational activities. In this case, the story begins with traditional indigenous educational practices, which, as Brown and Hiskett (1975) observed, still form part of the educational picture today as part of the informal dimension of current educational experience. Such practices would not have been uniform but varied considerably even within tribal groups, at clan level, or even within individual communities. The first incursions into what is now Sierra Leone were from the spread of Islamic colonization from the north introducing religious schools for the learning of the Koran. The distribution of these schools was not uniform. Some communities had several, others none. Much the same picture was painted by Christian incursions from the Atlantic coast. In addition to the spread of mission schools being uneven due to the capacity of different denominations being variable, there was also the issue of rivalry, so that some communities would have two or more competing schools while others had none. The pattern of Christian influence was made even more unbalanced by the settlement of freed slaves from the Americas after abolition of the slave trade and then emancipation. The newcomers were concentrated on, and near, the Freetown peninsula, and also enjoyed dedicated financial support for schooling, for example from the Lady Mico Trust. This led to the founding of elite schools in Freetown. These immigrants had no African culture or language, speaking instead a form of English known as Krio. Some of the institutions founded from the early nineteenth century onwards became prestigious internationally, such as Fourah Bay College (1827), the first university in sub-Saharan Africa. It became a constituent college of the University of Durham from 1876 to 1966, after which it formed part of the new University of Sierra Leone. Bo School, an elite boarding school for boys founded in 1906 for the sons of Paramount Chiefs, also became internationally renowned, drawing pupils from East, Central and Southern Africa. Meantime the Annie Walsh School for Girls was founded in Freetown as early as 1849. These prestigious institutions, based entirely on the English model, strongly influenced the nature of schooling in Sierra Leone throughout the colonial period and beyond.

The internal *political geography* of Sierra Leone further emphasized the dichotomy between the Christian and Islamic legacies as the Freetown peninsula, known as 'The Colony' became divided into parishes, each with a school, while the mainly Islamic interior was of a different status with an irregular scatter of relatively isolated mission schools. Unusually for a British colony, the colonial government took early interest in education alongside the missions, but a national system did not expand over the whole territory. Most of Sierra Leone was divided between chiefdoms, with tribal chiefs taking the initiative for the founding of schools. With this interest varying considerably from place to place the distribution of schools in relation to population continued to be extremely irregular. After independence in 1961, and especially under the dictatorships of Siaka Stevens and Joseph Momoh, the country descended into corruption which further intensified disparities in access to, and quality of, schooling as some districts were favoured, others not.

This was connected with the *economic geography* of the country as wealth-creating enterprises were concentrated in the urbanized Freetown peninsula, with much of the interior in a state of so-called 'subsistence affluence', there being mostly a landowning peasantry. Systems of land tenure and kinship are significant influences on educational chances in the majority rural populations of developing countries. This brings us to the decade of civil war from 1992–2002, which developed from a spin-over of the conflict in neighbouring Liberia to battles over the control of diamond and other mineral deposits and internecine tribal warfare. The main rebel forces, as they were known, gained much of the territory before the intervention of peace-keeping armies from the UK and West African countries eventually turned the tide, and relatively democratic government took over in 2002. It is a curious fact that the initial military coup ousting President Momoh in 1992 resulted in the return of international aid projects, including a World Bank nationwide basic education initiative. This was destroyed by the civil war and in any case neutered by its own agency's policy of structural adjustment of the economy.

Emerging from under all this is the enduring *social and cultural geography* of Sierra Leone with the inertia of its sharp urban/rural dichotomy epitomized by the Krio concentration in Freetown and the predominantly Islamic interior. The interest in education of many tribal chiefs has preserved basic schooling in the current state of national poverty, where central government is unable to fund and operate a national system. Devolution and community funding of schools have developed partly by default. However, a major legacy of the civil war is a massive displacement of population to Freetown, including many thousands of orphans and vulnerable children. So while the rural interior has returned to some extent to the traditional areas of about sixteen local languages, the Freetown peninsula hosts a massive melange of displaced cultures concerned with day-to-day survival alongside a reviving elite with international and global connections.

What now occurs in any locality in Sierra Leone is an amalgam of residual elements from the contributions described above to the educational realities on the ground today. They all play their part, from indigenous African educational survivals to the cybernetic capability of the university with its global connections. Over the past centuries and today, what happens on the ground has been subject to pressures on education at geographical scales from global to local, as illustrated in Figure 2.3.

LIVERPOOL JOHN MOORES UNIVERSITY
LEARNING SERVICES

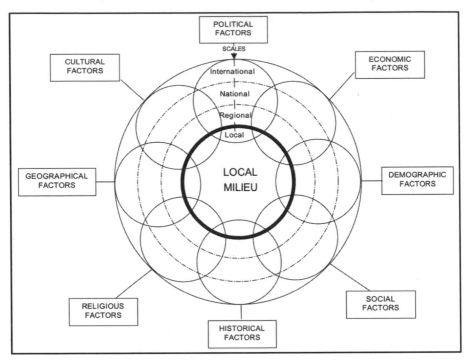

*Figure 2.3 Spatial scales and factors affecting education in any location*

The diagram shows how the various factors influencing the nature and delivery of education operate differentially at scales ranging from global to local. This can be illustrated with regard to Sierra Leone by taking the political and historical factors and comparing their educational influence at different times and scales, as in Table 2.1.

It is essential, at least to some degree, to comprehend the elements of past educational scenarios that contribute to the mix that constitutes the current context in every location. Failure to understand the complexities of local contexts lies behind the urgent need to make a humanitarian response to the needs of the people in any locality today. Table 2.1 has introduced a temporal dimension, and so we turn now to the temporal scale.

## Temporal scale

Any meaningful response to educational need must take account of temporal scale, that is to say the passage of time over which the provision occurs. It has already been noted that the likely most influential form of education, the informal, is lifelong, but scarcely taken into account by

| Scale | Global | International | National | Regional | Local |
|---|---|---|---|---|---|
| **Religious** | Christian/Muslim Interface | Christian/Islamic NGOs | Secular system | Religious/tribal interface | Particular external/traditional mix |
| **Historical** | Legacy of slave trades with Americas and Arab world | Legacy of British colonialism | 1990s civil war | Influence of tribal disparities | Residual legacies of the past |
| **Cultural** | Influence of Anglophone media and ICT | Pan-African and West African links | Creole Lingua Franca | Local language | Unique local cultural identity |
| **Social** | Modern sector values versus traditional | Links with Sierra Leonians elsewhere | Health issues Gender policy in law | Kinship systems and land tenure | Degree of maternal authority |
| **Economic** | Multilateral aid for education | Bilateral aid and international NGOs | National economic resources and budgets | Paramount Chiefs and schools | Community funding |
| **Geographical** | Location relative to global networks | West African and Commonwealth connections | Implications of physical and human geography | Internal political geography | Local milieu |
| **Democratic** | Global brain drain of the elite | Cross-national patterns of migration | Internal migration: IDPs and OVCs | Population change- urban/rural dichotomy | Unique local demographic identity |
| **Political** | Membership of UN agencies and World Bank | Changing bilateral relationships inc. Pan-African | Balance of democracy and corruption | Degree of decentralization and devolution | Degree of local power even if by default |

Table 2.1  Scales and factors affecting education in Sierra Leone

educators. Also noted above is the mismatch between the term of office of a politician with responsibility for education, and the length of time an individual takes to pass through the compulsory stage of most systems. A third temporal issue already alluded to is the imbalance between rates of educational change and economic change. This makes correspondence between curriculum and economy extremely difficult unless there is highly authoritarian centralized control over both, such as obtained in the former USSR or, somewhat differently, during the 'Cultural Revolution' in the People's Republic of China (PRC). Such a dictatorial approach offends the democratic imperatives of what is generally regarded as 'good government'. And then, as illustrated through the case of Sierra Leone, the educational history of a country leaves a residue from each stage of the experience that becomes part of the contemporary picture. If the contribution of every such part is not recognized, and the reason for its survival not understood, then any new initiative will face puzzling and apparently hidden problems.

The holistic notion of education as a humanitarian response, whether applied to existing and entrenched situations in developed countries, or to incomplete systems in poorer countries, or to an emergency, implies change. Except in the context of a fundamental political revolution, as in Russia in 1917, or a sudden and massive natural disaster such as the tsunami in Aceh, Indonesia in 2004, which razed whole towns to the ground, there is not normally a clear break in ongoing provision to provide a real opportunity for change. In the Russian case, a very high proportion of the population was illiterate at the time, which meant that, at least as far as formal education was concerned, there was a *tabula rasa*.

In most circumstances, introducing change will not work unless it is first ascertained in some detail 'where the target population is at'. This applies as much to any particular lesson in the classroom as it does to undertaking a project of educational development in a country like Sierra Leone. In the case of the classroom, the level of understanding at the beginning will be different for each pupil. In the case of the development project it will be necessary for a real understanding to be had of the range of residual elements of past educational experiences that contribute to the current situation. In both cases, understanding 'where people are at' will be difficult to determine, but if this is not achieved then the chances of success are severely compromised. Taking the time and making the determination to understand the existing situation, which must take into account all forms of education, is of the essence of education as a humanitarian response.

So the notion of any educational response to a perceived need implies a temporal dimension and a realistic assessment of what that should be. Emergency situations, by definition, demand a rapid response, but share with interventions in the mainstream the necessity for the seeds of sustainability to be sown at the outset. This is a vital fundamental principle along with the maintenance of support over the medium and long term. It takes a significant length of time for innovations to 'take' after being grafted. Very often in the case of the established mainstream the necessary degrees of support and of time are not maintained. They may be aborted by a change of minister of education or of an entire government. Political timescales, especially in democracies, are short. As short-term change follows short-term change, each leaves its legacy to add to the accumulated culture of education in any particular place. That place may be large in spatial or demographic terms or it may be very small, but the effect is the same, to make it more difficult for sustainability to be achieved. Figure 2.4 illustrates a range of timescales as applied to the locations of different human circumstances from margin to mainstream.

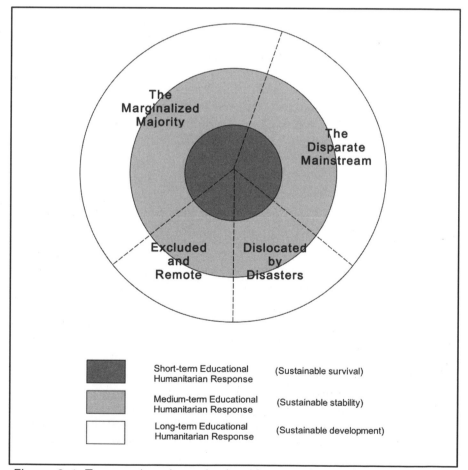

*Figure 2.4 Temporal scale and education as a humanitarian response*

Mainstreams imply convention, and this is not only true of established systems of formal education based on national cultures. It can also be true of large development agencies, whether multilateral or bilateral. Until the 1990s, development support to education was provided in terms of projects, each of which was provided with funding for a given period of time. This principle was replicated within each designated phase of the project, and the flow of financial support maintained, paused or withheld according to whether or not timeline schedules were met.

These schedules were drawn up in some detail, using business-derived log-frame methods to determine the meeting of targets at each stage and the triggering of the next phase of funding. Little latitude for flexibility was available, a key component of a humanitarian response, especially in the context of structural adjustment. Also, since projects had a fixed ending, almost always too early for the strands of sustainability to take root, there was little to show for the investment, financial or otherwise. Such projects are less common in the twenty-first century, unless for the construction of a finite facility. Instead, financial aid to education is fed into the mainstream system, in what is known as a sector-wide approach, such as primary schooling. This is maintained over much longer periods than those of projects, is subject to systems of accountability, and therefore has greater chances of engendering sustainability.

# The notion of cultural capacity

Education in all its forms is *culturally embedded*. In respect of the formal mode, and much of the non-formal, it is *politically provided* in terms both of funding and content. It has been argued above, that especially in the majority mainstream, a mismatch between culture and politics prevents a thoroughgoing humanitarian response to educational needs whether at the level of the individual, community or nation. This may well also apply when responding to the needs of the excluded, the marginalized and those subject to disasters, whether due to human or natural causes, or a mixture of both. But in these cases there may be a greater possibility of convergence due to the opportunity to rebuild in a different way, though such an opportunity is rarely taken due to the forces of politics and inertia at work. This may be the insistence of government that the 'situation ante' has to be restored because of the social-control function of the system, or it may be due to lack of imagination on the part of some or all parties concerned. Either way, it results in insufficient time being afforded to the consideration of something that would require a significant cultural adjustment as well as goodwill on all sides. Cultural adjustment is possible because culture is always changing, and this is recognized in the centrality of capacity-building to the development process. As Brock and Cammish (1997) have observed:

> The notion of capacity-building for institutional and operational development along systemic lines is well established. It is recognised as a necessary preparation for the absorption of increased levels of investment and recurrent operation – that is to say, for achieving sustainable development.
>
> (Brock and Cammish, 1997, 118)

Nonetheless, capacity-building is often unsuccessful because the cultural demands of such a process are not recognized, or if they are they are sidelined for political or economic reasons. In any case, capacity-building may not be for change, which is why the term 'systemic' is included in the statement above. In other words, cultural capacity has been overlooked, despite the fact that it is a necessary ingredient for capacity-building to be achieved. As Brock and Cammish (1997) go on to point out, this is not just a matter of culture, but also of time: 'This leads directly to the concept of *cultural capacity*, which is, we would suggest, the extent to which and the rate at which a society is capable of absorbing cultural change' (118).

This brings us back to the issue of scale. The power for sustainable development does not lie at the macro scale of governments and international agencies. Rather, the locus of power for change is at the level of family and community. It is latent at the local level, and especially in the cultural nature of relationships between the sexes.

# Gender

Of all the factors most universal in relation to tapping that latent stimulus for cultural capacity-building through a humanitarian response to educational development, gender must be the most fundamental. This is also connected to the issue of scale. It was noted above that the founding of the Annie Walsh school for girls in Sierra Leone in 1849 preceded that of the Bo school for boys by nearly half a century, and yet in the present day less than 50 per cent of girls of primary school age in that country are attending primary school. This is because of the scale and cultural locus of the earlier innovation, created for Krio Christian girls descended from freed slaves and focused in the capital, Freetown. Historically it has taken a long time for equal educational opportunities for girls and women to be addressed even in the more developed countries. In the mid nineteenth century the Krio elite of Sierra Leone was well connected with influential reformers in England where private or endowed schooling for elite girls was emerging. This led to university opportunities for privileged women from the 1870s, though in Oxford they were not allowed to gain degrees until the 1920s and in Cambridge not until 1948! Access was widened after the 1902 Education Act and the emergence of selective secondary schooling in grammar schools, many of which were founded in the inter-war period from 1919 to 1939. Even this was compromised by the nature of the selection process whereby the number 'passing' the Eleven Plus examination was determined by the number of places available in grammar schools. As mentioned above, for reasons of disparate historical legacy, such schools were more numerous in some areas than others, which was inequitable for both boys and girls. But on top of that, the number of grammar school places had to be approximately equal between the sexes. This further, and severely, curtailed the chances for girls, who in general achieved more highly at that age. So it was not until the mid 1960s, and the introduction of non-selective secondary schooling in most English LEAs, that a situation of near equal opportunity was reached, a century after the process began. This process was not so slow in all developed countries, but it is important to note that by the time further advances were gained through Western feminism from the 1960s onwards, these were built on a long effort of attrition on the part of, mostly female, activists, some of which took place even before the nineteenth century.

Turning to the situation in less developed countries, and especially the poorest, the EFA gender parity goal for primary school enrolment has already been missed and postponed to 2015. Even that is almost certainly unattainable. Since reaching equality of educational opportunity in gender terms is almost certainly the most widespread and fundamental humanitarian need, one might have afforded it a separate chapter in a book of this nature. After all, one of the strongest supporters of female educational opportunity, Professor Lalage Bown, has rightly observed that 'women are development' and 'no women, no development' (Bown, 1985). But to make gender a separate issue would be to deny its fundamental universality as a key element in the social and cultural contexts within which a humanitarian response to educational need has necessarily to function successfully. As LeVine and White (1986) pointed out in their seminal contribution to the influential Harvard Project on 'Human Potential and Its Realisation', the response to any basic educational innovation will depend on what they term 'the complex symbols that move men and women in diverse settings' (210). They go on to assert that it would not be appropriate to 'accept any interpretation of the motivating quality of those symbols that is not based on evidence concerning their cultural meanings' (210–11).

LeVine and White's volume contributing to the Harvard Project has the sub-title: 'The Cultural Basis of Educational Developments', which is another way of acknowledging the influence of non-formal and informal education. In subsistence farming communities wherein the majority of the world's population still reside, the relationship between the sexes at the level of the individual family is the key to decisions made about education. With the majority of such societies being patriarchal, with all that this implies in terms of kinship and relative wealth, the greater authority more often resides with the male head of household. This favours the allocation of scarce schooling opportunities to sons rather than daughters. The male partner may well have enjoyed some elementary schooling, but even in terms of indigenous traditional education will likely be advantaged over his female partner. Both may be very cautious in respect of innovation, since their family economy is one of survival, based on a socio-cultural structure that has proven over generations to have supported that modest goal. In the significant minority of subsistence societies that are matriarchal, such as the Ashanti in Ghana, due to the pressures on females in respect of child bearing and rearing, they may well still not have enjoyed access to schooling. But in both patriarchal and matriarchal circumstances the age–sex hierarchy that obtains in each locality will mediate the take up of any outside innovation such as schooling. Females know that the age–sex hierarchy provides a degree of modest security for them as they proceed through the years. The family lies at the heart of decision-making and is the context within which cultural change can be engendered. Anthropological evidence would suggest that the creation of a cultural climate supportive of educational take-up in the formal sense increases as the age of females at marriage rises, and a greater degree of equality between the partners is engendered. In other words the strength of maternal authority is increased.

Maternal authority is particularly strong, indeed unchallenged in the minority of locations where matrifocal situations exist, as traditionally in Jamaica and some other Caribbean societies where serial monogamy is common. This is where mothers hold the power of decision-making due to the absence of a long-term stable relationship, and instead experience a series of partners. Such mothers, having the power of authority by default, tend to support the education of their daughters strongly in a country where universal primary and secondary education is available throughout. In general, Jamaican girls outperform their male peers and gain more places in selective secondary schools and then university. This is also related to social class, so that middle-class Jamaican boys have a similar record of achievement to that of their sisters.

In the majority of poorer rural societies, however, enhancing maternal authority could be achieved by means of enhancing female literacy and income-generation capacity, both of which have to do with non-formal education. A major limitation to the efficacy of the introduction of formal primary schooling in poor rural societies has been the mismatch between that schooling and adult education, even supposing that the latter has been introduced at all. In all societies, developed or underdeveloped in the economic sense, strong parental support for the schooling of children is a key factor. In other words, a convergence between formal and informal education strengthens both. The great success of South Korea and other East and South-East Asian countries in PISA has a great deal to do with family, and especially maternal, support. It became apparent on further scrutiny that many Korean fifteen-year-olds spent more time in private sector coaching on the subjects tested than in school itself. This can be taken too far, of course, leading to undue stress, breakdown and even suicide, but in moderation parental support is a necessary support to meaningful learning. Unfortunately, in poor rural and urban communities, where the majority of the world's people still reside, the lack of adult education of a kind that can support children and young people in their learning is a strong influence on lack of progress. The culture of the school and the culture of the family are estranged.

A remarkable and well-known project in Bangladesh has done a great deal to overcome this problem. It is the Bangladesh Rural Advancement Committee project (BRAC). It has tried, with some success, to help create the type of family situation conducive to successful schooling in rural areas, and has been in operation for some three decades. A key element in this success was to concentrate initially on a form of education that would enhance the income-generating skills of rural women. This went on for at least a decade including both technical skills, such as weaving and cloth-making, and literacy for special needs, such as understanding memoranda of understanding and contracts to ensure their labours are properly rewarded. Once the capacity for income generation reached operational levels, male heads of household became more supportive. Their partners were able to use their newly acquired diffuse skills to argue for the children, especially girls, to go to school. Although not explicitly a gender project, the BRAC scheme required that, if a village established a school with project support, then 70 per cent of enrolment would be female until a gender balance had been achieved. Early in a new location, illiterate teenage girls were given the chance to enrol and often took it enthusiastically, frequently completing the five-year basic cycle in just two years and then becoming eligible for secondary school.

Another simple but fundamental innovation was to require the village community to build the school itself. This they did with the same materials and structures as their homes, so that the school did not look out of place. A frequent problem in other rural communities has been to erect an alien structure on the edge of a village so that the school, even when welcomed, did not feel part of the community, and neither did the teachers who were drafted into it by remote administrations. The BRAC scheme required that the teacher come from the local community, hopefully a woman with at least a little primary schooling. Such a teacher would be trusted by all parents, some of whom had been unwilling to entrust their children, especially girls, to a teacher, especially a male teacher, from outside. These local female volunteers received minimal training in the working of the scheme, the national primary curriculum, and a box of support materials. Project workers, male and female, would visit regularly to provide on-the-job training, advice and more materials. Finally, provided that the local community would ensure that the same number of days of schooling as required by national regulations would be guaranteed, they were allowed to coordinate school attendance with the needs of the local economy, and not keep to strict artificial term times.

So the BRAC scheme has worked by (1) understanding the significance of maternal authority; (2) comprehending the need to maintain this by operating positive discrimination in enrolment; (3) understanding the need for the hours and days of schooling to relate to local economic needs; (4) respecting local culture with regard to the security of girls; (5) connecting with the formal system so that those who have the ability to progress to secondary schooling are able to do so if it is available within reach or by boarding; and (6) making the village school with local materials and therefore part of the culture. Similar schemes have been developed elsewhere in Bangladesh and in other countries, but it is not yet the common experience. Its success began with the foresight to think of the change in cultural capacity that would be required, and to give sufficient time for it to be generated. Many factors bearing upon education had to be accommodated: geographical, economic, cultural, political and, most fundamentally, gender. It was, and continues to be a holistic and humanitarian response to the needs of the type of communities involved at this stage of their development.

## Summary

In this chapter it has been argued that the majority of the world's people have educational experiences that are inappropriate to realizing their potential, and that to a significant degree this is due to failure, individually and collectively, to see education as anything other than the formal mode. This in turn is due to governments seeing compulsory schooling only in terms of social control and investment in economic development, and failing to understand the intrinsically cultural basis of successful educational developments. A range of circumstances was discussed, from rare cases where education and culture are in harmony, through dysfunctional inclusive systems, ill-served minority groups, the marginalized, those temporarily disconnected due to disasters, those excluded by human action and finally those wavering between inclusion and exclusion. In all circumstances, the significance of scale, spatial and temporal, for understanding of context and culture needs to be comprehended and taken into account for meaningful development to be possible. A human rights approach is a step forward as it recognizes the imperatives of accommodating cultural diversity, all three forms of education as they inevitably interact, community participation, protection and flexibility. This brings us to the heart of development, which has to do with cultural capacity-building and its fundamental connection with gender relations. It also illustrates that education as a humanitarian response should be for everyone.

The discussion will now move on to consider the educational situation of most of the world's population, the excluded and marginalized majority.

# The Excluded and Marginalized Majority $\boxed{3}$

## Chapter outline

## Introduction

There is a fine line between exclusion and inclusion. It is not just a case of whether or not one is inside or outside a system of educational provision. We have seen above that it depends on what that system is for. As Richard Schaull so aptly puts it with regard to Paulo Freire:

> Education either functions as an instrument which is used to facilitate integration of the younger generation into the logic of the present system and bring about conformity or it becomes the practice of freedom, the means by which men and women deal critically and creatively with reality and discover how to participate in the transformation of their world.
>
> (Schaull, 1972)

The assertion that education as a humanitarian response is an essential approach to addressing the learning needs of all does not mean that their problems are all the same. It is obvious that the nature and the acuteness of the need ranges across a wide spectrum of conditions and situations that were illustrated in Figure 2.1 above. There are many overlaps between the seven categories listed there. For example, a minority group may also be refugees fleeing from conflict; it might be a travelling community, or a group oppressed or neglected within its own country; or all three. It is counter-productive to become embroiled in the minutiae of typologies and classifications. So for the next three chapters I propose to move from different degrees of marginalization and exclusion from the mainstream to situations arising from disasters, whether of human or natural causes, to disparities within the dysfunctional mainstream. There will still be many overlaps, but that is in the nature of a complex and dynamic global population with diverse educational circumstances and needs.

In dealing with the various groups and situations comprising the marginalized majority, the discussion will progress from the most extreme form of exclusion, slavery, to movement from marginalized to mainstream as is the case in some travelling communities.

# Slavery

This aspect of inhumanity has already been alluded to in the historical context with respect to educational support accompanying freed slaves from the Americas to West Africa, especially Sierra Leone. Historically, there have been few other examples connecting education and slavery in a positive way, such as the fashion of elite Romans to have educated Greek slaves to learn from, and the practice of the Caribbean colonial plantocracy of affording educational opportunity to the offspring of liaisons between planters and their slaves. This led to an educated Creole class that played a leading part in post-emancipation developments up to independence. But these are rare examples of hundreds of years ago and in any case did not benefit the majority of slaves. When slaves were transported from Africa to the Americas, they were deliberately separated from their tribal and linguistic kin in order to minimize the possibilities of organized rebellion. In other words, the most essential cultural component for forming a base for informal education, language, was destroyed.

It is a severe indictment of humankind that, in the early twenty-first century, a considerable amount of slavery still exists in the world. Approximately 20 million people worldwide are bought and sold, held captive and exploited. The United Kingdom has a greater share of contemporary slavery than most people realize. According to a 2007 report of the Joseph Rowntree Foundation:

> With the growth of globalisation and migration, it has become clear that modern forms of slavery are growing in the UK. This study attempts to map its extent and nature, reviewing the evidence on key areas of slavery in the UK, particularly forced labour, debt bondage, sexual slavery, and child trafficking and labour.

The report, based on research undertaken jointly with the Wilberforce Institute for the study of Slavery and Emancipation (WISE) of the University of Hull, in defining slavery recognizes three essential characteristics: (1) severe economic exploitation, (2) lack of a human rights framework, and (3) control by the prospect or reality of violence.

Figures are necessarily difficult to compile with any real degree of accuracy, but it is thought that about 500,000 of the 20 million worldwide have been trafficked into labour exploitation in developed countries, much of it in sex and/or drug trades. But this is dwarfed by a figure in excess of 200 million children worldwide engaged in illegal labour in conditions tantamount to slavery. We can add to that the many millions of women around the world, mostly in the poorest regions and countries, who for cultural reasons are denied access to education by their husbands. They would not normally be regarded as slaves, but in practice they are. Even some Bangladeshi women in the UK come into this category. They would be more likely to gain some education from the BRAC project in rural Bangladesh.

One could go on, but here the discussion is about education and slavery, where we can recognize two opposing situations. The first relates to attempts made by various humanitarian agencies to free those in slavery from their situation and introduce them to aspects of non-formal education that relate directly to their immediate needs. The second relates to the informal education they are receiving from the work they are doing. This will vary according to that work, and although a significant proportion are involved with sex or drugs, there are many who may be in illegal employment but are carrying out legal tasks for their captors. This is not to say that the informal learning they are experiencing is necessarily appropriate, but that it cannot be said that there is none.

The majority of those in slavery are either young or adult women, or working children. The two categories may well be connected in that so-called 'street children', or runaways, are often under the control of 'street adults' who train them in the sex or drug dealing trade and provide them with shelter and protection. They are rarely living on the streets in the conventional sense. It is an alternative society with its own informal education built in. In the context of British cities such children run into the thousands overall. Attempts to draw such children into, or back to, formal schooling often fall foul of the clashing roles of local social services, the police, and the NGOs that are working 'on the streets' to different ends. It is a delicate, often slow, non-formal educational process based on gaining trust and providing protection. Even in the rare cases where it works, the reluctance of the schools to cooperate given the individual control they have over admissions, negates progress. Clearly the issues of child labour and slavery overlap, but it is thought that the majority of working children are not slaves and so need to be considered within the marginalized group of humanity known as vulnerable children and young people.

# Orphans and vulnerable children (OVCs)

This category not only overlaps with slavery but also with the context of disasters, and the emergency responses to human needs, including education, that follow. 'Education and Disasters' is the theme of Chapter 4, but despite the large numbers of children and young people involved in disasters, the majority of vulnerable children exist neither in slavery nor in the context of emergency responses. Rather, they are part of the world's mainstream populations, both urban and rural, and as such it is difficult to define, quantify and understand their educational experiences and needs. Such children exist in considerable numbers across the whole global population from the most developed to the least developed nations. Orphans are obviously different by definition from the majority of vulnerable children, but tend to be more identifiable in more developed nations which have, in respect of both governmental and non-governmental agencies, been able to respond to gather data and support responses to their needs. However, one category of orphans that is widespread and numerous within the marginalized majority is that of those whose parents have died of HIV/AIDS. This pandemic ranks as a disaster, and as such will be discussed in the following chapter.

Within the more developed world the issue of vulnerable children, and orphans in particular, has become particularly visible and concerning in some of the countries of Eastern Europe. Of these nations, some, but not all, have emerged from the control of the former USSR, either from being part of the Soviet federation or by being within its strong sphere of influence and control. Others, such as the Balkan states arising from the break-up of the former Yugoslavia, have suffered from relatively recent violent conflict. Ukraine, a former republic within the USSR, which became independent again in 1991, as referred to in Chapter 1, has experienced mixed fortunes since then. It no longer has the favoured situation it enjoyed within the USSR, and while the majority of the people favour the freedom they now have, they have suffered in some ways from the different economic model now obtaining. This has engendered much greater disparity across the country and a widening gap between a rich minority, mainly in Kiev, and a majority ranging from relative to absolute poverty.

According to a study currently in progress by academics at the Kirovograd State Pedagogical University on educational responses to orphans and street children in Ukraine, 10 per cent of children in the country are homeless, orphaned or abandoned. The national Institute of Family and Youth has estimated that there are nearly 100,000 crisis families. The authorities operate sanctions by taking away parental rights and removing children from such families. Accurate figures are difficult to come by, but it is thought that near to a quarter of a million children are either orphans or abandoned by their families. The national authorities have set up 'Internats' for the accommodation of abandoned children, but all are overcrowded and increased capacity is needed. Many of the street children in Ukraine are runaways from institutions which in any case they have to leave on reaching the age of seventeen, when it is estimated that 50 per cent of leavers are recruited into crime, including prostitution and trafficking, a significant number taken into Western European cities. The Government of Ukraine pronounced the year 2006 to be 'The Year of the Defence of Children's Rights' and even before then sought to support facilities and staff to offer some education to institutionalized children and young people. UNICEF is active in the country, along with about fifty other smaller agencies or charities, some of which deal with educational support in the broadest sense.

Despite the genuine efforts being made to reach and support children and young people in need in Ukraine, there are still many thousands of so-called 'street children', some of whom are orphans, others not; some are working children, others are just destitute, including 'railway children'.

Returning to the broad international scene, it is obviously necessary to clarify the meaning and implications of these rather vague categories. Without a more sophisticated understanding of this complex problem it is unlikely that interventions, as in education, will be appropriate. They might even damage the prospects of children escaping these circumstances. Because the family connection, if any, is of prime significance, especially maternal support, it is possible to differentiate between children (1) working on the streets but living with their families; (2) on the street but with only sporadic and limited family links; (3) without any family connection. In broad global terms it is thought that about 70 per cent of such children have some family connection and that a similar proportion do attend school, albeit irregularly. This pattern has lead to a two-fold classification of these children as being either 'on the street', the majority, or 'of the street', the minority.

Latin America, and especially Brazil, has long been seen as having the most dramatic images of street children of various kinds, usually associated with 'shanty towns' or *favellas*. These are illegal settlements, which, by definition, are excluded from public education provision and whose occupants are obviously too poor to afford the private option. Many *favella* communities do operate their own schools though only a minority attend, and the curriculum followed is not necessarily close to that in operation in public and private schools in the wider community. Nonetheless, there is some non-formal education going on, as well as non-formal support for some adults. It was this type of support for adult literacy in the equivalent (*barrios*) of Chile under Salvador Allende that attracted the displeasure of Augusto Pinochet and was brought to an abrupt end by his coup in 1973. Similarly, in Brazil the work of Paulo Freire led to his deportation and denigration by the Brazilian authorities.

Education itself can be a cause of children coming out of school due to the rigidities of the promotion system from one grade to the next in many countries, including Brazil where only about one-third of children entering the first grade of schooling complete the primary cycle. The example given in the 2010 GMR Summary is Nicaragua with 27 per cent. When a child is required to repeat a whole year, this is often beyond the means of most parents in developing countries and their children are withdrawn, many becoming 'working children'. So in most locations a direct connection with formal schooling is not the solution. There has to be a broader non-formal response linked to such survival imperatives as: (1) keeping the home and family support at least connected; (2) acquiring basic skills for possible employment including self employment; (3) promoting awareness of contextual dangers such as disease, crime and even brutality on the part of official authorities. A significant proportion of children in 'street' circumstances are quasi adults, due, for example, to early marriage or lack of parental presence to help look after younger siblings. They need these types of support before they can get anywhere near the modern economy skills offered in formal education.

In many 'shanty' and other poverty stricken urban locations in Asia and Africa as well as Latin America informal and non-formal educational support comes from the work of voluntary efforts by charitable and religious organizations. Such efforts provide safe houses, street educators and communal education workshops. They need to be sustained beyond childhood and adolescence to have any lasting effect, but resources are extremely limited compared to those going into EFA at primary level.

## Extreme poverty and the marginalized majority

While the numbers of orphans and vulnerable children are considerable in absolute terms, and worldwide in occurrence, the majority of children in the world who are either not at school at all, or who are attending intermittently, far outnumber the OVCs. These are the predominantly rural children in the major zones of underdevelopment in sub-Saharan Africa, Asia, Latin America and the tropical island zones of the Caribbean, South Pacific and Indian oceans. These children, together with the young adults, parents and grandparents in their communities, still form the majority of the world's population where the rate of increase in numbers is keeping it that way. By the standards of the urbanized societies of the developed nations, where the term 'relative poverty' has become employed in response to a widening gap between the richer and the poorer, this rural majority experiences real, or even extreme, poverty. This is why most multilateral and bilateral development agencies, such as the UK government's Department for International Development (DfID), have 'poverty reduction' as their paramount objective. In DfID's Research Paper No. 48, the objective was to examine the relationship between the imperatives of economic survival and educational opportunity. The authors, from the University of Bristol and the University of Dar es Salaam, refer to the children in question as 'the lost children', and recognize them as the majority of the country's children. Although this study is wrapped around by the usual caveats of the academic world – it is called a 'preliminary study' with 'tentative' results and recommendations – it is in fact exemplary in method and comes forward with some telling findings and recommendations. It is realistic in saying that 'Children will be required to contribute to the local informal economy in a substantial way for a long time to come' (DfID, 2003, 67). This is in no small way due to the fact that such populations are 'young' with over 50 per cent under eighteen years of age, and a health scenario where HIV/AIDS is making that ratio worse. They rightly say that 'we need to adopt and adapt education to accommodate the work they must inevitably carry out' (ibid.), and that:

Given that the life of the child in Tanzania is closer to that of an adult in metropolitan societies, it is, therefore, sensible to look at the techniques that have been developed for working adults to access further education, rather than solely trying to emulate Western style school education.

(DfID, 2003a, 68)

The authors rightly conclude that realizing such an objective will require radical changes to the way in which formal schooling is currently delivered. The periods of time when schools are supposed to be in operation (i.e. the school year), the selection of days on which to open within that time, and the relevance of the curriculum to the economy would all require the devolution of decision-making power to local communities.

Such a conclusion is not likely to recommend itself to any central government with its interest in controlling all of these things. Despite its evident realism, common sense and clear humanitarian response to child, community and national need, it risked going the way of the later Cambridge Primary Review (2009) in England referred to in Chapter 1. Politicians do, however, have a way of rejecting anything sensible that they hadn't thought of themselves only to unearth it later and claim the credit for it. The world can only hope. In such communities around the world the continued application of dysfunctional systems only serves to help perpetuate poverty. Indeed, in the same way, at a higher level in more developed countries such as the USA and UK, formal systems are not responding either to what is required in terms of operational numeracy and literacy. It is not merely a question of acquiring technical skills, but also to do with creating a cultural capacity for change within which an appropriate formal schooling can play its part. That is what lies behind the quotation above from the Tanzania study, and it requires a radical new mindset to inform both national governments and international development agencies.

The 2010 GMR, *Reaching the Marginalized*, shows that since the turn of the millennium and the Dakar Accord there has been considerable advance in the number of enrolments in primary schooling across the developing world. There is also evidence of some closing of the gender gap in this respect. But for these people, the silent majority, could this not even be counterproductive? In the words of the conclusion of the 2003 DfID Tanzania report: 'To some extent, (formal) education will exacerbate this situation in the short term' (67); that is to say, until the socio-economic culture has developed sufficiently to absorb the products of the formal system. This requires a close correspondence between curriculum and economy, which is extremely difficult to attain. In addition to a suitable core promoting literacy and numeracy, including ICT, there would have to be components of a liberal education and sufficient flexibility to resonate with the local socio-economic culture. Emphasizing core technical skills over all else, as encouraged by international surveys like TIMMS and PISA, is not enough. No country in the world has yet reached that point, which is one of the reasons why education is a global concern. Figure 3.1 illustrates the interconnection of three overlapping dimensions of any formal curriculum that would have to be present to have a chance of being appropriate to the learning needs in any locality. It would have the potential to contribute to the growth of cultural capacity necessary for dynamic and sustainable progress from survival to meaningful development for the marginalized majority.

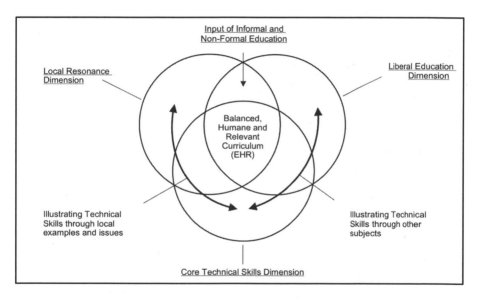

*Fig. 3.1 Essential components of a relevant curriculum*

# Teachers

Education, whether formal, non-formal or informal, implies learning, and learning implies teaching, whether that be intentional or involuntary. Everyone is likely to be acting as a teacher every day, whether intended or not, especially in the nebulous and expansive world of informal education. Very small children pose problems for their parents or older siblings, which have to be solved. Parents engender linguistic development in their offspring from birth, even though this may be achieved inadvertently rather than systematically. In traditional societies there are sophisticated practices for imparting knowledge and skills required to make the *rite de passage* from adolescence into adulthood. The training for this is often not parental but conducted by a designated adult. The adolescents may well have had some formal schooling, but that adult is just as much a teacher as those encountered in school. There may be elements of magic, symbolism, ritual and religion in these processes and they will be related to the culture of the society, its integrity and survival. The idea that there is no equivalent in so-called modern industrialized societies would be wide of the mark. It may appear much more chaotic and unregulated by comparison, but two particular groups have considerable influence from this stage and onwards: the peer group and the 'high priests' of celebrity and the media. They are influential teachers in the informal mode of learning, just as much as parents and family. In traditional societies such as in rural Tanzania, both the local and external versions will be in operation and competition through the globalized penetration of electronic information and ICT, making the informal world of learning even more complex. There are many teachers involved but some may be distant and come from other cultures. Nonetheless, their efficacy may well be greater than that of teachers in school, unless the formal sector embraces and integrates them.

Unfortunately, this is rarely the case. Those teachers working in schools for the marginalized majority in developing countries who have been trained have often had an experience derived from alien cultures. It has come down as part of the bag and baggage of metropolitan legacy, sometimes through direct colonial administration, or through Christian missions. Either way, the entry requirements, programme structure and qualifications awarded simply replicated those of the colonial power. Because these teacher training colleges often preceded universities in colonial territories, for example by over a century in Jamaica, they became a stepping stone to universities in the metropole or to occupations with a higher status than teaching, such as the civil service or banks. But even disregarding that, many were spectacularly dysfunctional. Because, in such situations, secondary schooling was, and often still is, enjoyed by a minority of students, most teacher training colleges were established for preparing to work in primary schools. There are a number of issues to consider: staffing, gaining entry, the programme of initial training and qualification, preparation for and supervision of teaching practice, in-service training and further qualifications.

Entry qualifications were set as near as possible to those obtaining in the teacher training programmes of, say, England. Because secondary schools had also inherited colonial models this would often mean five GCE

O levels. Such an attainment was very hard to achieve and likely only by a minority from urban-based secondary schools. The majority would be male students, though colleges were often single-sex and some were for women. The programmes followed mirrored those of metropolitan colleges, comprising three roughly equal components: academic study of main subjects, education theory and practice, and teaching practice in schools. The qualifications related to the staffing of such colleges on the academic and training side also replicated the metropole in that at least a first degree would be required. So from the outset, primary teacher training colleges were staffed by the minority who had degrees but had not necessarily taught in school. They were only capable of dealing with the academic study of their subject, and in most cases not its application to the primary classroom: that is to say, for example, they were educated in mathematics, but not in how to teach mathematics. Supervision of teaching practice may well have been conducted by college lecturers with no school-teaching experience at all. This clearly dysfunctional situation is described in rather measured terms in the report of one of a number of international projects that have attempted over recent decades to promote its reform.

> Teacher education appears to be one of the most conservative parts of many education systems. It seldom is the source of curriculum innovation, theorised pedagogy or radical reconceptualisation of professional learning. It often lags behind schools in the adoption of new practice and patterns of learning and teaching. This is a signifier that political will and bureaucratic courage may be needed for the implementation of real changes designed to improve efficiency and effectiveness.
>
> (DfID, 2003b, xxv)

This comes from the DfID research report on the MUSTER project, researching teacher education in five countries: Ghana, Lesotho, Malawi, Trinidad and Tobago, and South Africa. The research is exemplary and comes to some very telling conclusions and recommendations. While the study revealed the modest academic backgrounds of most new trainees, it also commented on their relative closeness to the socio-economic backgrounds of the majority of pupils they would teach. This could be an advantage so long as the academic demands of the programme did not lead to a disconnection with, or even disregard of, this affective quality. Teacher trainers rarely, it seems, appreciated the value of this familiarity with the informal and non-formal educational components of their pupils' socio-economic contexts. This led, the project observed, to a disregard of the stock of learning their often unqualified charges brought to the training experience. Indeed, a significant proportion of trainees had worked as unqualified teachers and had relevant experience to bring to a reflective dimension of training had it existed. To refer back to an essential first step in any successful teaching programme, indeed in every single lesson or lecture, it is essential to ascertain 'where the students are at'. Failure to do so will produce a disconnection between the formal curriculum and the non-formal and informal curricula, and will render the formal dysfunctional. Figure 3.1 relates just as much to what goes on in primary teacher training programmes as it does to primary or secondary school curricula.

With respect to the selection of candidates for such programmes, the MUSTER project report commends the 'On-the-Job Training' (OJT) mode of Trinidad and Tobago, which is institutionalized, and recommends its wider application thus:

> The development of OJT-like schemes has several attractions – trainees can be selected partly on the basis of their performance over time, rather than initial academic qualifications; trainees contribute to reducing teacher shortages through the work they do; managed OJT could greatly enrich the skills and competencies of those entering training.
>
> (DfID, 2003b, 198)

A similar proposal was made as part of the World Bank Basic Education Project in Sierra Leone in the mid 1990s, where the majority of primary school teachers were untrained. A key recommendation was that the considerable pool of recently retired headteachers would enhance the supervision of the practicum, along with the existing head of each school involved. Academic staff of the teacher training colleges were to be used largely to upgrade the knowledge base of trainees during intensive periods of attendance at the colleges during school vacations. In many sub-Saharan African countries, and other parts of the 'developing world' of the marginalized majority, such a pool of potentially active ex-headteachers exists, their experience and skills untapped. They inevitably have pension problems and so turn to other income-generating activities and are lost to education. Unfortunately, the project in question went the way of much else in education during the civil war in Sierra Leone.

While the MUSTER project illuminated many problems in primary teacher education programmes in the countries concerned, and made a number of important recommendations for their resolution, the Teacher Education in sub-Saharan Africa (TESSA) programme, led by Professor

Bob Moon, seeks to roll out reform in this sector across the decade 2005–15. As such, it is making a significant contribution to supporting the global effort to reach MDG 2, the realization of universal primary education (UPE) by 2015. TESSA's consortium structure involving a number of partners also addresses the objectives of MDG 8, the development of global partnerships for development. Table 3.1 indicates the key characteristics of TESSA and its partnership composition.

---

### A. Summary of the TESSA Programme

TESSA is a research and development programme, providing a bank of multimedia resources, in traditional text and on-line formats that teacher educators and others can use to provide school-based education and training for teachers in the education sector. TESSA is:

1     A partnership programme that will contribute to the education of the millions of teachers needed for the expanding basic education sector in sub-Saharan Africa.

2     Planned to utilize the best African and international expertise in supporting locally based needs and users.

3     A flexible resource directly aimed at local school based and supported education and training.

4     Modular in format and focused on classroom practice in the key areas of literacy, numeracy, primary science and personal and health issues in education.

5     'Open content' free to the users and suitable for incorporation into a wide range of programmes.

6     Designed for versioning to diverse cultures and linguistic communities.

7     Using both traditional materials and a range of information and communication technologies (ICTs).

### B. TESSA Consortium partners

- African Virtual University.
- BBC World Service Trust.
- Commonwealth of Learning.
- Open University of Tanzania.
- Open University (UK) – Coordinating Institution.

*Table 3.1 The Teacher Education in sub-Saharan Africa programme*

Apart from improving the quality of the teacher training experience in sub-Saharan Africa (SSA), the TESSA programme of research and development is seeking to combat two problems it reckons to be more prevalent there than in rural Asia and Latin America: teacher migration and para-teachers. The former can only be reversed by conditions of teaching improving considerably, but the latter is a serious threat to the quality of the teaching force as it involves very brief periods of initial training before recognition. By contrast, well-managed OJT schemes are sustainable and rooted in the locality of the trainee.

TESSA has the potential to make a difference because of the spatial and temporal scales of its operation. Active across nine SSA countries, it also employs forms of ICT that can be accessed even in remote areas. Mobile phones for in-service support are becoming widespread. Apart from enabling the enhancement of teacher professional development, they also support dynamic connections with the realities of the local socio-economic and cultural milieu. This in turn enables schooling to make a contribution to local cultural capacity-building, without which development is seriously constrained. In particular it helps connect with vital non-formal educational work in the field of health with which several of the MDGs are concerned, especially, but not excusively with reducing and preventing HIV/AIDS as well as living with it.

The design, operation and achievements of TESSA to date are indicative of what is meant by education as a humanitarian response because it seeks to provide a training experience for teachers that is mindful of context. The limitations bearing upon primary teachers are many, but one that is of prime importance is the very low level of literacy among the majority of adults in most local communities of the marginalized majority. This does not seem to manifest itself in a lack of belief in schooling as such, but rather, somewhat perversely, in a lack of confidence in its ability to benefit the family and community in the short term. This disconnection is at least in part due to the lack of correspondence between the formal curriculum of the school and the informal curriculum that informs community survival. One of the reasons for this is the massive discrepancy in funding as between formal, especially primary, education and non-formal, especially adult, education. This is mainly due to the thrust for EFA, which the 2010 GMR indicates to be progressing steadily if enrolments are a true indicator. Intermittent attendance and progressive wastage are less encouraging, and they are due to parental decision. Clearly governments and the international community believe this is the way forward, but it needs a parallel commitment to technical, vocational and adult non-formal education to enable the potential contribution of schooling to social and economic development to be realized.

# Literacy, adult and non-formal education

From its inception in 1945, UNESCO saw the acquisition of literacy as fundamental to helping the world's marginalized majority – a larger proportion of the total than it is now – to overcome grinding poverty. Joseph Watras identifies four characteristics of that programme that may well have worked against its realization. They are, he states, as follows:

> the imposition of modern scientific cultures on indigenous cultures, the manipulation of indigenous people, the masking of cultural traits, and the view of failure as an indication of the need for increased efforts.
>
> (Watras, 2010, 221)

In hindsight, things have moved forward a long way since then. Declarations of human rights, principles such as 'ownership', and techniques such as participatory rural appraisal have helped to engender partnerships for development. But in line with the fourth problem point in the quotation above, following the end of the programme of fundamental education, UNESCO embarked on programmes of mass literacy launched in the 1960s with reference to all three major zones of underdevelopment: Africa, Asia and Latin America. Their massive scale completely overlooked the basic issue, namely that motivation to become literate has to be engendered from the need to overcome very local frustrations, even down to the scale of the individual and the family. The issue of female literacy and its crucial role in engendering levels of maternal authority affecting family decisions on the schooling, or not, of children has already been noted above. The local imperative had long since been illustrated by the mobile 'Cultural Missions' of Jose Vasoncelas, first minister of education in post-revolutionary Mexico, in the 1920s which continued into the twenty-first century.

In 1980, the inaugural edition of the *International Journal of Educational Development* arose out of a meeting in London called to review the outcomes of the targets of UNESCO's 1960s regional initiatives towards universal adult literacy. They were nowhere reached, though mass literacy projects continued in various locations, failing to take account of new perspectives on literacy developed by radical thinkers, such as Brian Street, since the 1970s.

In terms of widespread radical initiatives in adult literacy, a significant breakthrough occurred in 1993 with the launch of what has proved to be the highly successful Reflect programme. Developed by the NGO ActionAid, and especially David Archer, it was trialled in Bangladesh, El Salvador and Uganda for two years before going global. Its success is based on core principles which are applied through small local groups. These principles are summarized in Table 3.2.

| Core principle | Summary |
| --- | --- |
| Power and Voice | To strengthen the capacity of individuals to communicate in a meaningful way through practical use. |
| A Political Process | Reflect is not neutral. It is there to help people assert their rights. Reflect aligns with the poorest and most marginalized. |
| A Democratic Space | Creating a space where all voices are given equal weight. This has to be counter-cultural by challenging power and stratification. |
| An Intensive and Extensive Process | Reflect groups meet on average for two years, several times each week. Intensive and regular contact is important. |
| Grounded in Existing Knowledge | Respect of existing knowledge is fundamental, but such knowledge can be challenged, and new information utilized. |
| Linking Reflection and Action | Continual cycle of reflection and action for the purpose of change. |
| Using Participatory Tools | Using a wide range of tools to assist participation, e.g. maps, diagrams, role-play, song, dance, video and photography. |
| Power Awareness | Power and stratification as the focus of reflection to help change unsuitable relationships using structural analysis. |
| Coherence and Self-Organization | Reflect operates systematically and applies all its principles to itself. This encourages self-organization by groups. |

*Table 3.2 Reflect: the core principles*

Reflect describes itself as 'an innovative approach to adult learning and social change which fuses the theories of Paulo Freire with the methodologies of participatory rural appraisal' (Reflect, n.d., 5). Now used by hundreds of organizations, mostly NGOs, it is promoting meaningful adult literacy and learning in more than seventy countries. It is salutary that the innovative thinking and work of Paulo Freire, begun in north-east Brazil in the 1960s but confined in practice to Cuba, Chile and Guinea-Bissau by his exile from his homeland, should have found a home in the Reflect initiative. One of the strengths of Reflect is its sustainability, which has been enhanced by critical evaluation from the outset. In 2001, an independent review of thirteen evaluations across ten countries was conducted. It showed clearly the empowerment potential of its approach to literacy acquisition, the resulting growth in self-esteem, and the positive impact on gender relations. Since then there have been evaluations in many locations and a review of sixteen of these was published in 2009.

Along with the evident upward trend of primary schooling towards EFA, at least in terms of enrolment, there has been a growth in adult literacy. There is, however, significant divergence between these trends in respect of (1) their local relevance and (2) the funding involved. Consequently they do not converge sufficiently to satisfy the degree of integration of the forms of education envisaged in Figure 3.1. This dichotomy is exemplified by the quotation from Paulo Freire at the beginning of this chapter as well as by one of the founding fathers of comparative education, Isaac Kandel, in his submission to UNESCO's fundamental education proposition in 1945. According to Watras (2010, 223), Kandel observed that acquiring literacy in school simply enabled people to avoid the everyday tasks of their community whereas schooling should everywhere contribute locally to engender what he called a humane society. Well over half a century later, seldom do we see formal schooling acting as a humanitarian response to the present and peculiar needs of society in any particular location because it is locked into a national curriculum leading to national examinations and certification.

Literacy is not just an issue in the less developed countries. It is a contemporary concern of all developed countries as is well illustrated by the 'Family Literacy and Learning' approaches in the UK, USA and a number of other countries. As their name implies, these are mutually supporting approaches designed to encourage parents and children to work together to the same end: to address the need for both to acquire both literacy and numeracy. Projects have been developed in the UK for over thirty years, concentrating on areas where the problem is most acute – in disadvantaged families often with a single parent. The majority of children with poor reading and communication skills have parents who are barely literate. Monitoring of programmes designed to address this family problem stresses the importance of promoting the opportunity to read, write and discuss as well as finding ways of recognizing progress and rewarding it, then connecting with everyday interactions within the family, finally leading on to local and community issues. Both local and national government have been supportive of such initiatives, sometimes linking with methods and materials used in primary and secondary school. This is good practice as it also helps the teachers in schools to relate the formal curriculum to local circumstances. The pragmatic task of relating literacy acquisition to observable benefit is a major indicator of progress, but relies heavily on family learning practitioners. They need to have the awareness and skills to recognize the importance of relevant literacies to cultural capacity-building through confidence, so as to steer their adult charges into non-formal learning opportunities and more meaningful and gainful employment where such exists.

Non-formal learning constitutes a very significant proportion of educational activity everywhere, but in the world of the marginalized majority it is especially significant. Virtually throughout the post-millennium conflict zone that is Afghanistan, a sustained effort by UNESCO and Japanese aid has done a remarkable job not only in literacy acquisition but also in developing and sustaining locally relevant knowledge for local security and at least a degree of development. In less fraught but still challenging circumstances, innumerable NGOs, local, national and international, work with local communities throughout the mainly rural populations of South Asia, sub-Saharan Africa and Latin America to effect real practical benefits to ease the struggle for survival. In educational terms, many such operations have both learnt from, and been inspired by, the legacy of E.F. Schumacher. His 1973 book *Small is Beautiful*, said to be one of the top 100 most influential books since 1945, highlighted the fundamental significance of the local context if anything by way of development is to be achieved. The sub-title of the same book – 'A Study of Economics as if People Mattered' – is equally telling. It implies, rightly, that decisions regarding the funding of development, including education, are normally made at the macro level and relate to the political control function.

In addition to *Small is Beautiful*, and in order to demonstrate his approach in practice, Schumacher founded the NGO Intermediate Technology, based near Rugby in England. This is still one of the most innovative actors in the field of non-formal education among the marginalized majority, and now goes by the name of Practical Action. The main aim is to help poor communities, through appropriate technology, to overcome immediate problems relating to energy, shelter, transport, water, food, climate, information and disaster risk reduction. The NGO does this in a range of countries through interventions that introduce intermediate technology capabilities in, for example, micro-hydro electric power, building sustainable homes, installing ropeways and roads, harvesting rainwater, assisting agro-processing, combating desertification, introducing manageable modes of ICT for education, and planning for response to potential disasters. These things are carried out in the field but are also supported by getting involved in formal education, especially primary and secondary schooling, in the UK as well as in the poor communities themselves. Practical Action acts as a teacher through advocacy to encourage multilateral agencies and donor country governments to focus on the underlying causes of poverty through: (1) providing practical solutions to local technological problems; (2) providing support for teachers in donor and recipient countries to be able to focus on the key issues of underdevelopment; and (3) disseminating examples of good practice as lessons of the fundamental nature of success at the grassroots for any further development to be possible. This is the bedrock of sustainability, without which secure foundations for any meaningful innovation are impossible. It is the key overlap between non-formal, informal and formal modes of education that is provided by exemplary NGOs such as ActionAid and Practical Action that lies at the heart of education as a humanitarian response.

| Activities | Field | Principles |
|---|---|---|
| Micro-hydro<br>Solar<br>Wind<br>Biogas | Energy | 1  We help reduce the vulnerability of poor people affected by natural disasters, conflict and environmental degradation. |
| Building<br>Housing<br>Planning | Homes | |
| Ropeways<br>Trailers<br>Roads | Transport | 2  We help poor people to make a better living – by enabling producers to improve their production, processing and marketing. |
| Rainwater<br>Harvesting<br>Irrigation | Water | |
| Farming<br>Agroprocessing<br>Biodiversity | Food/ecology | 3  We help poor communities gain access to basic services – water, sanitation, housing and electricity. |
| Coping with<br>desertification | Climate<br>change | |
| Computers,<br>Radio,<br>Video podcasts | ICTs and<br>education | 4  We help poor communities respond to the challenges of new technologies, helping them to access effective technologies that can change lives forever. |
| Floods,<br>Droughts,<br>Earthquakes | Disaster<br>risk<br>reduction | |

*Table 3.3 Activities and principles of the NGO Practical Action (based on information from Practical Action, 2010)*

It is important to note that three exemplars of teacher education and training (TESSA), adult literacy enhancement (Reflect) and intermediate technology (Practical Action), while rooting their efforts firmly in local cultures, societies and economies, all connect directly with ICT at appropriate points in their interaction with poor communities. In so doing they are invoking the powerful connection between global and local scales that is inherent in globalization. This should not be a problem provided that valuable traditional understandings and interpretations of relationships between human populations and their environments are respected. Unfortunately, in many other interventions this is often not the case and the opportunity for learning from local conventional wisdom is lost. This is particularly sensitive in relation to those on or beyond the fringe of the margins – indigenous peoples.

# Indigenous peoples

The term indigenous is not easy to define. It is not just an issue of language. There are hundreds of languages in the developing countries, the world of the marginalized majority, and the issue of literacy acquisition has to take account of that, as the Reflect programme certainly does. But the numerous linguistic minorities in such large intensely multilingual countries as Nigeria and India are not normally thought of as any more indigenous than larger linguistic groups. Yet the United Nations Organization has a Permanent Forum on Indigenous Issues and recognizes education as being one of its key areas of concern. Some groups recognized as indigenous are in more developed countries, such as the 'First Nations Peoples' of Canada. They are not the same as other minority groups contributing to diversity and disparity in the mainstream, and as such receive distinctive recognition as far as education is concerned.

What is particularly relevant about the nature of the educational dimension of indigenous cultures for the concept of education as a humanitarian response is its holistic character. Recognition of the educational needs of indigenous peoples still living in their ancestral lands, or of those who find themselves one of many minorities within a mainstream, is not just a question of human rights. It is also a question of the contribution indigenous understanding of the natural environment can make to a better world future for all. As Ole Henrik Magga (2004) explains:

> For indigenous peoples, it is the knowledge of the interconnectedness of all that was, that is and that will be – the vast mosaic of life

and spirit and land/water forms, of which we are an intricate part. It encompasses all that is known as Traditional Knowledge. Indigenous cultural heritage involves a holistic approach, where traditions and knowledge are embodied in songs, stories and designs as well as in the land and the environment – the intangible interlinked with the tangible. For Indigenous peoples, sacred sites and intangible cultural heritage are intimately woven together and cannot be easily separated. These allow us to balance development with our environment, which we have occupied since time immemorial. This knowledge indeed forms the central pillars of our culture; pillars that also sustain the Earth. Deviation from this knowledge has grave consequences for the world and for human kind.

(Magga, 2004, 7)

As is self-evident, such deviation has unfortunately been the story and legacy of colonialism in its various forms, including its educational dimension. Instead of our learning from indigenous wisdom, that fundamental knowledge has been ignored by modern education itself, especially formal schooling. This has been aided by the religious component of colonization. Martin Carnoy invoked the phrase 'education as cultural imperialism'. All cultures have many components, but the two most prominent are probably language and religion. Both were front-line tools of colonialism, coming together in the role played by both Christianity and Islam in the establishment of schools. Nonetheless, as the quotation from Brown and Hiskett in Chapter 2 above indicated, indigenous African education owed nothing to these major cultural incursions, and seems to have survived them. This is not only a good thing in itself, but means that if we are wise we can benefit our own modern cultures by helping to protect indigenous education and learning from it. UNESCO, in particular, and many of its individual national members are trying to do this before it is too late. NGOs are also at the forefront of such efforts, which often involve components of the formal system such as universities where the role of anthropologists can be central. Such polar cross-connections between the extremes of formal education (university) and informal education (indigenous) lie at the heart of a holistic employment of education as a humanitarian response and are mediated and delivered through non-formal initiatives and programmes.

A good example of this type of initiative is the work of the Programme for the Promotion and Capacity-building in the Amazon (PROCAM) with the indigenous Ashaninka in Eastern Peru where non-formal education is described as 'an educational experience for children, youth adults and elders, connected to a process of local and community development'. This is outlined in Table 3.4.

---

- The fundamental bases and principles of the Ashaninka worldview

- The fundamental bases of individual and collective identity and self-esteem-or what it means to be Ashaninka

- The Ashaninka's own perception and definition of what is presumed to be 'Ashaninka culture'

- The rediscovery of ancestral cultural practices and the current status of artistic-cultural practices

- The identification of knowledge, techniques and skills involved in diverse artistic cultural practices

- Identification of production processes and the main components of socio-educational and cultural practices

- Identification and analysis of the main factors which threaten their cultural identity, as well as those that strengthen and enhance it

- Recognition and organization of the main educational and cultural agents

- Collective recovery and re-creation of knowledge and practices linked to: the protection and balanced exploitation of eco-systems; the management and organization of territorial space; social, political and cultural organizations and institutions, and the bases of Ashaninka leadership

---

*Table 3.4 Fundamentals of curriculum for an indigenous people: the Ashaninka of Amazonian Peru*

*Source: Martinez, 2004, 205–16*

In the example of the 'Ashaninka Creators' the non-formal mode is being utilized to assist the development of local indigenous people, while recognizing and including the unique symbiotic relationship their communities have with their environment. That natural environment happens to be one of the key resources on which the future of human life on the Earth depends. Indigenous knowledge and education in this case lies at the heart of our survival, but it can also be of fundamental importance in cases where indigenous populations are neglected, even oppressed, minorities in economically advanced countries such as Australia, New Zealand, Russia and the USA. Here again non-formal education projects promoting intercultural understanding are helping to progress the social and economic prospects of the national mainstream and indigenous minorities alike. But in order for such initiatives to lead to sustainable development over generations, it is vital that both primary and secondary schools are included and play key roles.

As such schools form the compulsory sector of formal education in most countries, because that is where the political control function of education by governments is exercised, this imperative is largely ignored or at best marginalized. One global-scale category of indigenous people who have a range of degrees of connection between their education and that of mainstream compulsory formal schooling are travelling communities.

## Travelling communities

Travelling, traditionally termed nomadic, communities represent about 300 million people throughout the world. They move through a wide range of environments from very harsh, such as the Arctic wastes and the Gobi desert, to the urban areas of industrialized nations. Their relationship to formal education is often marginal and ambivalent. Most share a fundamental connection with the natural world because they are also indigenous peoples. But their relationship with formal education, because of their travelling, makes them a distinctively different group. In order to illustrate the commonalities and differences, three examples of travelling communities will be mentioned here: Gypsies and Travellers in the UK and Ireland; the Rabaris of the Ran of Kutch, north-west India; and the Negev Bedouin of Israel.

> The receptionist looked at me with disdain when I walked into Suffolk College asking to enrol. Their access course for mature students didn't have any entry requirements as such, but the receptionist warned me it was an advanced intensive course, and there seemed to be a blank space under 'educational history' on my application form. When I explained that I wasn't a dropout, I just hadn't been to school, she looked even more scornful. I was 22 and had never spent a day in a classroom in my life; an alien concept for many people but common in Gypsy and Traveller families. There are more than 100,000 nomadic travellers and Gypsies in the UK, and 200,000 who live in permanent housing'. Many, like me, never attend school, while others are illiterate because formal education is not a priority in our culture.
>
> (Freeman, 2009)

This opening extract from Roxy Freeman's article 'My Gypsy Childhood' subtly illustrates both marginalization and ambivalence. She goes on to say that: 'Our education was learning about wildlife and nature, how to cook and how to survive. By the age of eight or nine I could light a fire, cook dinner for a family of 10 and knew how to bake bread on an open fire.'

There is little data on Gypsies and Travellers in the UK, but their levels of literacy are known to be extremely low. It was not until the 1960s that efforts were made to offer them places in formal schools. This broad category is normally recognized as comprising a number of distinct groups: (1) 'Romany Gypsies', also known as 'Romanies' and 'English Gypsies' but who travel in South Wales as well; (2) the Kales in north Wales; (3) 'Scottish Travellers', on both sides of the border; (4) 'Irish Travellers' or 'Tinkers', also in the UK. All these can be traced back to at least the sixteenth century, their descendants having migrated from northern India soon after the end of the first millennium. Another major traveller group in the UK are the Roma, who entered much later from east-central Europe in the 1930s. Their movement was accelerated by Nazi persecution, then events in Hungary in the late 1950s and then again by the accession of a number of countries in that region to membership of the European Union in 2004. The widespread diaspora of the Roma has been such as to lead to UN recognition as a distinct ethnic group in 1979.

All the above-mentioned traveller groups in the UK exhibit certain common views of nomadic groups worldwide towards education. They see it as internal to their own cultures which are all family based. That is the economic unit, and what has to be learnt to sustain the way of life is generated within it informally. They are by definition self-employed, adaptable, multi-skilled and self-sufficient. As Juliet McCaffery (2009) puts it: 'The data suggest that Gypsies and Travellers do not regard a lack of mainstream education and low levels of literacy as a deficit and many continue to regard mainstream education as a threat to their culture and lifestyle' (644). She goes on to show that where they do see literacy, in particular, as an asset it is with regard to the frequent challenges they face from the power of mainstream society. The oral foundations of their own culture enable them to utilize modern elements of ICT to respond strongly and effectively to attempts to control them. In many cases, they learn such skills from their children, who may attend formal schooling even if intermittently. Indeed, McCaffery ends on an optimistic note, suggesting that: 'Multi-modal communicative practices and skill in literacy discourse can contribute to future harmonisation instead of assimilation' (655).

The view of formal schooling as an asset in dealing with hostile actions from the dominant sedentary mainstream and its politics appears to be a feature in nomadic societies as far apart as the cattle herders of the Sahel and the horse breeders of the Gobi desert. These are pastoral nomads whose economies are necessarily less adaptable than those of the travellers in highly urbanized and industrialized European settings. They face different dilemmas, as is well illustrated by Caroline Dyer (2001). She observes that pastoral nomads are among the most marginalized peoples of all. They may get some special support from national or local governments as in Nigeria, Eritrea and Mongolia, but in the case of the Rabaris of Kutch in north-west India, whom she has researched for over a decade with Archana Choksi, that is not the case. The government favours a policy of sedentarization which the Rabaris oppose, but their way of life has been progressively challenged by factors ranging from: (1) the partition between modern India and Pakistan creating political barriers in 1947 to (2) the degradation of the natural environment by India's modern economic boom. This political boundary also cuts across their traditional migration routes. As amongst other travelling peoples, the family is the economic as well as the social unit and the Rabaris have their own informal education to respond to its replication generation by generation. Rabari culture has a strong religious dimension allied to the economy. As Caroline Dyer puts it:

> For them, animal husbandry has a religious foundation which is largely indifferent to profit and loss considerations. Rabaris devoutly believe that their lives, and those of their animals, are in the hands of the Mother Goddess (mataji); and that they are privileged to be the guardians of her animals during their mortal existence, rather than their owners. Before they set out, religious rites are performed to commend the migration to mataji's care, and if animals fall sick or die, Rabaris interpret this as mataji's call, and are diffident about the use of medicine as a response. In common with other nomadic groups, too, values of herd growth outweigh economical means–ends calculations.
>
> (Dyer, 2001, 322)

As Dyer and Choksi found in the field, any attempt to adapt formal acquisition of literacy and numeracy skills to their ongoing nomadic economy failed because they had no meaning in this cultural context. However, with their whole culture threatened by local bureaucrats – who, in any case the Rabaris regard as of a lower class or caste – they, like the Gypsy Travellers in the UK, see literacy as a valuable tool in arguing their case for survival. So, as the thrust for EFA spreads across India with a succession of internationally supported UPE projects, they have begun to enrol their children, especially boys, in school. Because they have seen this resulting in cultural dislocation between those who go to school and those who do not, the Rabaris have come to favour their own boarding schools within which their unique culture is encapsulated. Although, unlike the Gypsies and Travellers in the UK and Europe, the Rabaris can see their traditional livelihood and culture being destroyed, they also see that acquisition of literacy and numeracy through formal schooling can enable them to challenge authoritarian attempts to make them sedentary. But these processes, literacy programmes and EFA alike, carry ideological 'baggage'. As Dyer concludes: 'development through education for minority groups demands that the value positions underlying EFA be articulated and contextualised' (325–6) – that is to say, looking towards education as a humanitarian response.

The dilemmas of a traditional nomadic group have been taken a stage further in respect of education by the Bedouin of the Negev who are mostly in Israel. They number about 140,000 and are a component of Arab Palestinian society within the borders of Israel. According to Richard Ratcliffe (2007), education has been a political issue for the Bedouin since 1990. He observes that their case illustrates 'the fundamental ambiguity of education's political role in state–society relations' (163). This is the political factor at work, probably the most influential of all the factors as affecting the content and delivery of educational services. It represents the intrinsically coercive dimension of formal educational provision, as opposed to its enlightening and liberating potential.

The Bedouin in the Negev have become largely sedentary, but like other nomadic groups who have settled and become recipients of the formal schooling system, they require that their cultural identity be taken into account within the nature of that provision. Although part of the Israel five-through-eighteen school system, they are separated from the mainstream by their language and internal political geographical boundaries. The facilities they are provided with are sub-standard, and for Arab teachers within Israel a posting to the Bedouin schools is the least desirable option. Consequently these schools have low-quality teaching staff, low achievement and high dropout. However, the acquisition of effective levels of literacy enabled them to contest this situation by concentrating on campaigns to improve the technical quality of the provision. Through a sustained effort from 1994 onwards they gained real technical improvements, but external control mechanisms remained. Cultural capacity for change has increased through the greater participation of girls and women, and their enhanced advocacy skills have had some positive effect. Ratcliffe sums up the situation in the following terms:

the political role of education among the Negev Bedouin is neither oppressive nor libratory. It is both, and crucially it is both always and at the same time. It is this ambiguity which makes education such an interesting lens for looking at the interaction of competing political agendas.

(Ratcliffe, 2007, 179)

In terms of education as a humanitarian response, the numerous travelling and nomadic communities of the world exhibit almost the whole spectrum from complete exclusion – due to remoteness and/or mutual consent – to complete inclusion but on contested terms.

# Summary

Reaching the excluded and the marginalized actually involves educational initiatives in relation to the majority of the world's people, the marginalized majority. Within this vast number, certain distinctive situations exist that have been discussed above: (1) those in slavery – many more than is popularly imagined; (2) orphans and vulnerable children – a growing category in less and well developed countries alike; (3) teachers in school who are barely more literate and numerate than their pupils, but on whom more depends than any other category save one – parents; (4) illiterate adults relying mainly on non-formal efforts from NGOs; and (5) indigenous and travelling communities with their dichotomous educational imperatives – the survival of their own cultures through informal means within the family, and contesting their independence from political authority by acquisition of sufficient of that authority's formal literacy.

In all these categories considerable efforts with regard to educational provision are being made with different degrees of dysfunction. The task is monumental. It has been argued above that to have a chance of overcoming any degree of dysfunction all three forms of education need to be involved. The most influential, the informal, will be in operation anyway as part of the culture of any human group or community. This will happen even in prison. If the informal dimension is not engaged, which is nearly always the case, then even the best efforts of schooling will not be as effective as they should be. Schooling is being strongly promoted, with the best motives, through the EFA imperative of the international community. In practice, this means UPE, with much less attention being paid to the secondary and tertiary sectors, which will not be able to play their full part unless the primary sector is effective. That in turn depends on teacher quality and adult education, especially appropriate literacy acquisition. In the world of the marginalized majority, the contribution of non-formal education to these two imperatives is crucial. Three examples of good practice in this regard were mentioned: the TESSA programme bringing together all three forms of education in its approach to teacher training; the Reflect programme of adult literacy which commences from 'where they are at', which is crucial; and Practical Action which utilizes modern technology in developing local economies. All three have been successful because they recognize that the capacity for education is culturally embedded and that efforts to develop must be in accord with cultural capacity. If they are not, then dysfunction will exist and progress constrained.

Both in respect of the marginalized, mainly rural, majority of the world's population and the mainstream education systems of the industrialized countries, there are very significant numbers of people dislocated from their normal educational experiences by disasters of various kinds. Chapter 4 is therefore concerned with 'Education and Disasters'.

# Education and Disasters

## Introduction

'Education and Disasters' is not the same as 'Education in Emergencies', though it subsumes this conventional term which has come into use in the past decade or two in relation to humanitarian responses to both natural and 'man-made' events and will indeed be a major concern of this chapter. But it is necessary first to take a broader canvas in both time and space to gain a wider perspective on the ways disasters can affect education, and not always for the worse. There is also often an overlap between the human and the natural dimensions of disasters as they influence education.

## Education and war: hot and cold

Wars are obviously disasters, but they would appear to be a generic feature of human behaviour over thousands of years. Few other animal species kill for reasons other than for food, and if they do it is nowhere near the scale of human annihilation. There is also a propensity for cruelty, including torture, that seems to be peculiarly human, or rather, inhumane. There are many ways in which wars have affected and still affect education in all its three forms. Among these are: (1) profound changes in the political geography of large and small areas; (2) destruction of educational facilities and staff; (3) changes to demographic patterns; (4) gender-related issues; (5) the portrayal of wars in textbooks and other instructional media; (6) their influence on informal education and mythology; (7) education in the military; (8) accelerated scientific and technological development; (9) educational reform. None of these things are new, but until the relatively recent development of a formal interest in 'education in emergencies', they have not figured significantly in the mainstream education literature and they need to do so. First, however, it is helpful to take a broader view in temporal and spatial scale.

Some aspects of the changing *political geography* of Europe can serve to illustrate the first point, because boundaries enclose regulated spaces within which formal education is provided and controlled. Since the European model of education has come to dominate the global pattern of formal education structures, we can begin with the extent of the Roman Empire in Europe and the resultant division into Romance, Germanic and Slavonic language areas. Language is the bedrock of culture and the main force in informal education. The decision of King Alfred to replace the Latin legacy of the Romans with the emergent English of the Saxons had a massive and permanent influence on education, despite the subsequent invasion and control of the French-speaking Normans. A few centuries later the support of the vernacular (German) by Martin Luther and Philip Melanchthon, and the spread of the Lutheran revolution, further curtailed the territorial influence of the Latin-based Catholic regimes and their educational interests. Napoleon Bonaparte not only reformed the political and administrative structure of French education, he also played a key role in rationalizing the kaleidoscope of over 300 German mini-states into thirty-seven major states which subsequently became a unified Germany with both federal and provincial education authorities. After the 1914–18 war came numerous boundary changes, which saw the creation of new nations in Europe, such as Czechoslovakia and Yugoslavia, and in the Middle East, where, for example, the modern nation of Iraq was formed. Plans were laid for the creation of Israel in Palestine, which did not in the event materialize until 1947. The legacies of the creation of these two new polities nearly a century ago, including for education, are among the most conflict-related in the early twenty-first century.

After 1945, most of Eastern Europe, including East Germany, was taken over by the USSR, which imposed its Marxist/Leninist ideology and the model of the ten-year polytechnical school. All these upheavals had implications for the education systems of Europe: changing areas of jurisdiction; languages of instruction; curriculum content, related texts and qualifications. Then in 1990 came the collapse of the Soviet Union and the emergence of a new Eastern Europe. Not only were the occupied countries free to redevelop their systems, there were also some boundary changes and the old Czechoslovakia split into two: the Czech Republic and Slovakia. At the same time Yugoslavia imploded and former polities emerged from eighty years before – for example, Slovenia, Croatia, Bosnia-Herzegovina and Serbia – each with their own new systems. Former republics of the USSR such as Latvia, Lithuania, Estonia, Belarus and Ukraine, were also free to reform their education systems. Meanwhile, in Western Europe the European Union had been created, and from 2004 several countries of Eastern Europe completed the accession process, thereby entering into educational opportunities and regulations in further and higher education. While the EU, now comprising twenty-seven member states, unlike most of the earlier developments, did not involve coercion, its raison d'être was part humanitarian – to avoid future conflict.

In addition to the Soviet occupation of much of Eastern Europe for nearly fifty years, there was also the shorter post-1945 occupation of West Germany by France, the UK and the USSR, and of Japan by the USA. These occupations had some effect on the reform of formal education systems in Germany and Japan, but as everywhere, education was culturally embedded in both and it re-emerged on its own terms. In the German case, it had to overcome the profound internal effects of Nazi education reforms as well. Understanding the role of political geography, a dynamic and changeable framework within which national systems of education are politically delivered, is fundamental to responding to educational issues that are conflict-related.

The *destruction of educational facilities*, along with the extermination of teachers and professors, is another legacy of war and occupation. When peace and freedom come along it is not always easy simply to carry on as before. The reconstruction of buildings and educational materials may produce an improvement, but many teachers may have been agents of the oppression and cannot be allowed to continue. This was the case in the early 1990s in the former East Germany where a large number of teachers proved unacceptable in the new context of reunification.

Intellectuals are often the target of violent reform, especially if it is of the military and/or fascist variety. This was the case, for example, in Nazi

Germany, and more recently in Chile after the 1973 military coup under Pinochet. Those that have not already been exterminated flee the country, often as refugees. They do not necessarily return, having made new lives in host countries happy to benefit from their talents and skills. Major conflicts on the scale of wars are still occurring in the new millennium most notably in Iraq and Afghanistan. Both have seen the persecution and flight of teachers and professors, and the destruction of educational facilities including priceless artworks and unique cultural treasures.

What, if any, has been the humanitarian response to educational upheavals due to war? In occupied Germany after 1945, three of the respective occupying powers in their discreet zones attempted to impose reforms in keeping with their own ideologies and systems. In the American zone, high-school democracy was the theme; in the French zone, the lycée with a strong philosophical foundation; in the Soviet zone, the ten-year polytechnical school. In the British zone, there was no plan of imposition but the selective grammar school model fitted best with the Gymnasium tradition by default. The pre-Nazi roots of German education soon showed through in all four sectors but the British lack of an imposed model proved, even if it was by default, a more humane response. These historic examples hold lessons for contemporary attempts to reconstruct and reform education after violent conflict.

*Demographic change* due to war comes in several ways that relate to education. The most obvious is through the increase in the death rate, especially of young adult males. This leads to a dearth of males throughout the life of that generation, and sometimes the next, as with the French *classes creuses* following the 1914–18 war and in the Soviet Union after the 1939–45 war. In the latter case, this is sometimes said to be a factor in the ongoing instability of family structures that has led to an unusual proportion of orphans and vulnerable children, as mentioned above in relation to Ukraine. Mass extermination or genocide will have obvious demographic effects. These may have a global resonance such as in the case of the Holocaust and subsequent further diaspora of surviving Jewish individuals and communities. More recently, and related to more localized conflicts across the globe, some including genocide, there has been the growing number of refugees, asylum seekers and internally displaced people. Much as in the past, flows of refugees often include a disproportionate number of well-educated and skilled people. Related to the issue of political geography is migration due to national boundaries shifting, so that people find themselves in another country without actually having moved. This has obvious implications for their education. A further and less discussed issue is the return of large numbers of military personnel after a major conflict. In England after the 1939–45 war, the return of demobilized servicemen coincided with the arrival of universal secondary education, and soon after that, the impact on primary-school enrolments of a boom in the birth rate. This meant an unprecedented expansion of the teacher-training sector, which later had to be rapidly contracted. Return from conflict is not always a positive experience for individuals and their families. Psychological problems such as trauma can render the former servicemen's potential contribution to the skills base of the society much reduced and also have negative effects on their children's prospects.

*Gender-related education issues* also occur in response to situations of war. Women may gain access to areas of gainful employment previously the traditional preserve of men. Some of these would be in non-combatant occupations within the armed forces, or even in some cases combatant ones. Others would be opportunities for skills acquisition through non-formal training and in professional roles in civil society, and in companies in the manufacturing and service industries. Post-war, many of these roles would be likely to be taken back by men, but the seeds of female opportunity and capability in these fields will have been sown. There is little doubt that the last global conflict of 1939–45 hastened the educational and employment opportunities of women, building on the pioneer efforts of feminist activists before and after the 1914–18 war. Not all war-related activities during those conflicts proved beneficial to women. For example, those who worked in munitions factories during the 1914–18 war were exposed to harmful materials, especially cordite, which had severe and harmful health consequences. The situation of women and girls in more recent and localized violent conflicts in less developed countries has not been enhanced in any way. They have borne an even greater economic and social burden than before, and been the victims of widespread and violent abuse leading to more lasting health consequences, especially HIV/AIDS contracted through rape.

*Textbooks* and other instructional materials often refer to past wars in a very partial way. They may totally ignore their country's defeats or at best treat them minimally. They may mention, but not in appropriate proportion, the contribution of allies to a victory and the price they paid in human lives. An example of this is the minimal coverage of the role of the USSR in the 1939–45 war in 'Western' school textbooks during the Cold War period. Even in the twenty-first century, few people appreciate that Soviet casualties numbered more than all others on both sides combined. In history curricula, conflicts, conquests and warlike leaders tend to be highlighted more than scientific inventors and humanitarian activists. All this has to do with the national political control function of formal schooling.

The *influence on informal education of major conflicts* is massive and long-lasting. Like all aspects of informal education, its contribution to understanding and perception is much greater than either the formal or non-formal modes of learning. From children's comics to blockbuster movies, the images and stereotypes involved build on an already ingrained mythological understanding that dwarfs the factual reality. From time to time there will be coverage of a humanitarian action, as in the movie *Schindler's List*, but these stories are outgunned, as it were, by action blockbusters.

Like the textbooks, depending on where the movie is made, and for which major audience it is intended, the positive role of the military of that country will dominate to the exclusion of others. For example, three allied countries took part in the crucial Normandy landings in the 1939–45 war, but a massively successful movie some fifty years after the event excluded all but the American forces. But probably even more influential is the informal educational influence of learning within the family about major conflicts such as the 1939–45 war, passed on generation by generation by a kind of educational osmosis. This can be reinforced in contemporary terms by national media coverage of contemporary wars. So just as the precise number of British military fatalities informs daily television news bulletins in 2010, the larger number of American dead is hardly ever mentioned. On the other side of the Atlantic, the reverse is the case. These imbalances are a function of nationalism, though rarely formally intended as such. Formal schooling in the shape of national systems and centralized curricula is also a function of nationalism. Member states of the European Union are happy to collaborate on higher educational convergence, such as through the Bologna Process, and also on technical and vocational education related to skilled worker migration, but are careful to safeguard their control over the compulsory sector of primary and secondary schooling. The seeds of what is now the European Union, sown in the 1950s with a prime aim of replacing conflict with co-operation, have not flourished in the formal schooling of the majority of member states. The so-called European dimension of the curriculum, encouraging the notion of being a citizen of Europe, is ineffective at best and marginalized at worst. Education as a humanitarian response needs to address the problems of those who cannot access schooling, but it also needs to deal with marginalization and imbalance within the formal curriculum.

*Education within the military* is an important component of non-formal education. In addition to combat skills, both genders in the armed forces of most countries in the world receive a great deal of technical and diffuse education in their initial and in-service training. This not only enables them to maximize their potential in the military context, including on active service, it also contributes to their capacity for meaningful employment after rejoining civil society. At the time of the last global war of 1939–45, a substantial range of texts were prepared by geographers and anthropologists to educate the British officers at least about the cultures and economies of the societies in whose territories they might well be fighting. In a more overtly humanitarian way, contemporary military personnel are trained to understand as far as possible the societies they encounter. In both Iraq and Afghanistan, front-line troops have gained an even greater understanding of local societies informally. In some cases they have been involved in humanitarian reconstruction, and on their return home have been able to help to educate both formally and informally from their first-hand experience. But this depends on whether the formal and non-formal sectors seek to engage them in this way.

Major conflicts tend to *accelerate scientific and technological* innovation that can contribute to subsequent social and economic development. Two innovations from the 1939–45 war that are commonplace now, albeit much refined, are the jet engine and radar. Decoding of secret signals speeded up computing, and more productive agricultural techniques were tested. On the downside, of course, the weapons of war also became more sophisticated and deadly, though some of that technology later made its benign contribution to the well-being of society at large – such as developments in military aircraft benefiting civil aviation.

*Educational reform* tends to be associated with major international conflicts. As mentioned above, schools tend to be blamed for military failures, but system-wide reforms also follow. With respect to England and Wales, defeat in the Boer War was a contributing factor to the 1902 Education Act, though the first national Board of Education had recently been established in 1899. The Act created local education authorities, rationalized the compulsory elementary sector and created a highly selective secondary sector of grammar schools. Partly as a result of the 1914–18 world war, the 1918 Education Act established the school-leaving age at fourteen and went some way towards the provision of 'central schools' for those who had failed to gain selection to grammar schools. However, many local authorities failed to create such schools, and it was not until the 1944 Education Act, stimulated by the Second World War, that universal secondary education was legislated for, and as a result the school leaving age was raised to fifteen in 1947. Similar relationships between major conflict and educational reform have occurred in other countries.

As we move on to consider the humanitarian response to both man-made and natural contemporary disasters, we do well to remember past conflicts and natural disasters on a global scale and the humanitarian benefits that have developed as a result, albeit often by default.

# Multilateral and bilateral agencies and NGOs

The failure of the League of Nations, set up after the 1914–18 war to help prevent another global disaster, the 1939–45 war, stimulated the creation of global international institutions such as the World Bank Group and the United Nations Organization. The former, based in Washington DC and owing much to American initiative, aimed to prevent national economies in difficulties from collapsing, and to help finance social and economic development in the poorer countries of the world through loan agreements. Related regional development banks were set up: the African Development Bank in Abidjan, the Asian Development Bank in Manila, the Inter-American Development Bank in Washington DC and the European Bank of Reconstruction in London, as well as the Islamic Development Bank in Jeddah.

The United Nations Organization is based in a variety of locations and has a more wide-ranging brief; it acts among other things as a development agency. It has a number of components that relate directly to educational development. These are the United Nations Educational, Scientific and Cultural Organization (UNESCO) and the International Institute for Educational Planning (IIEP), both in Paris, and the United Nations University (UNU) in Tokyo. It also includes other agencies that have education among their concerns, such as the United Nations Children's Fund (UNICEF) and the United Nations Development Programme (UNDP) both in New York, the United Nations High Commissioner for Refugees (UNHCR) in Geneva, the United Nations Development Fund for Women (UNIFEM) in New York, the World Health Organization (WHO) and the International Labour Organization (ILO), both in Geneva.

Another major multilateral agency with interests in educational development worldwide and with its rationale deriving from the last global war is the European Union (EU). One of its divisions (DGs) in Brussels, that relating to African, Pacific and Caribbean (APC) countries, is devoted entirely to promoting and supporting development. Member states contribute part of their overseas development budgets to joint EU programmes in the world of the marginalized majority.

International development ministries exist in the governmental machinery of most of the richer nations and these too characteristically derive from post-1945 decisions to engage in interdependent development. In 2002, such countries agreed internationally on the target of 0.7 per cent of national income to be assigned to international development aid. Each set their own scheduled date for reaching this target, but according to the Organisation for Economic Co-operation and Development (OECD), in 2009 only five had yet reached it, as shown in Table 4.1.

| Country | Percentage of National Income | International Development Agency |
|---------|------------------------------|--------------------------------|
| Sweden | 1.12 | SIDA |
| Norway | 1.06 | NORAD |
| Luxembourg | 1.01 | LuxDev |
| Denmark | 0.88 | DANIDA |
| Netherlands | 0.82 | NIDC |
| Belgium | 0.55 | BPPDC |
| Finland | 0.54 | DIDC |
| Ireland | 0.54 | Irish Aid |
| UK | 0.52 | DFID |
| Switzerland | 0.47 | SDC |
| France | 0.46 | AFD |
| Spain | 0.46 | AECI |
| Germany | 0.35 | KFW and GTZ |
| Canada | 0.30 | CIDA and IDRC |
| Austria | 0.30 | ADA |
| Australia | 0.29 | AusAID |
| New Zealand | 0.29 | NZAid |
| Portugal | 0.23 | IPAD |
| USA | 0.20 | USAID and IAF |
| Greece | 0.19 | MFA |
| Japan | 0.18 | JICA |
| Italy | 0.16 | IDCP |

*Table 4.1  Official development assistance 2007/8*

Source: Derived from OECD information, 2009

Of course, the percentages of national income do not relate to the actual amount of financial aid donated, as the USA and Japan are among the most generous in absolute terms. According to the OECD, 2008 was a peak year for international development assistance to date, and it remains to be seen whether the global financial crisis that occurred at that time will cause a decline overall. Some donor countries, including the UK, have pledged to safeguard their current commitments and remain on target to reach the 0.7 per cent of national wealth. Recipient countries number well over a hundred but there is a significant concentration in the top ten, as Table 4.2 shows.

| Country | Millions of $US | Percentage of global aid | Percentage of global aid |
|---|---|---|---|
| Iraq | 9462 | | |
| Afghanistan | 3475 | | |
| China | 2601 | 22% | |
| Indonesia | 2543 | | |
| India | 2262 | | 31% |
| Viet Nam | 1745 | | |
| Sudan | 1743 | | |
| Tanzania | 1603 | | |
| Ethiopia | 1551 | | |
| Cameroon | 1396 | | |

*Table 4.2  Top ten recipients of official development assistance funding 2007/8*

*Source: Derived from OECD information, 2009*

The concentration on two countries at the time of writing still occupied by foreign forces – in one case (Iraq) after a recent war and in the other (Afghanistan) during an ongoing one – is striking and further illustrates the close relationship between major wars and redevelopment, including education. Also striking is the concentration of aid given to the two most rapidly developing major economies in the world, China and India. This illustrates the major factor at work: the political. Between China and

India in the list is Indonesia, a genuinely poor country with the largest Islamic population in the world. Vietnam is in many ways similar to its Indo-Chinese neighbours Laos and Cambodia, but it is much higher on the recipient list than they are, most likely again with political (post-war and post-colonial) considerations to the fore. Sudan is the country within which the largest example of internally displaced people in the world exists.

While noting the influence of the political and the strategic in decisions to offer international assistance funds for development, it must also be recognized that the proportion of total aid designated for education is minimal.

NGOs may receive some of their income from multilateral and bilateral agencies, with all that this implies, but they also gain from public donations. Some are philanthropic and/or charitable foundations and receive donations from the general public. They are part of civil society but to some degree constrained by the political factor both in their own locations and in the countries in which they support humanitarian and development work.

The most long-standing NGOs are probably the Christian churches, whose history, as mentioned above, is closely related to the evolution of national systems of education, especially the European nation states. They were part and parcel of a major global act of aggression and territorial acquisition, European colonialism, which had profound educational implications in all regions of the developing world: Latin America, Asia, sub-Saharan Africa and the tropical island zones of the Caribbean, Indian Ocean and South Pacific. Ever since the end of the last global war in 1945, and the rise of the development business, the range of Christian churches has continued to make a significant contribution to education, especially formal schooling, in many of the countries that gained political independence during that period. Major Christian NGOs are at work, such as Christian Aid and Caritas, as well as Islamic NGOs, such as the Aga Khan Foundation.

Another global NGO that arose from the 1939–45 war is Oxfam. Founded in 1942 in Oxford by a group of Quakers and other activists to relieve famine in Greece, it was initially called the Oxford Committee for Famine Relief. Now, in 2010, the NGO has the title of Oxfam International and is a global confederation of fourteen organizations with more than 3,000 partners in over a hundred countries. The largest component is Oxfam UK, which has about 6,000 employees worldwide. Oxfam's core aims are still famine relief and poverty reduction, on which it works through non-formal education, both technical (e.g. enhancing water supply) and diffuse (e.g. through literacy acquisition and community development). The focus is on work with young people, most of whom have minimal schooling, if any, to enable them to contribute to the development of their local community. The scale is right, and all ages can benefit. Oxfam UK also promotes 'Education for Global Citizenship' in UK schools with materials appropriate for all ages from five to eighteen.

There are thousands of NGOs in the world making an invaluable contribution to education as a humanitarian response by filling gaps and making the vital connections between the different forms of education. The fact that education is normally only one of their concerns reflects their realism and enhances their potential contributions to social and economic development. Most of those mentioned above arose from major wars or their immediate aftermath. Others will be included in discussions below on particular themes in this chapter and in the following chapter on 'Disparities in the Mainstream'.

# Education and emergencies: situations of conflict and post-conflict

Thus far in this chapter the fundamental influences of major conflicts on aspects of educational legacy, negative and positive, have been outlined. This is because the seeds of many of the current responses to disasters as far as education is concerned can be found in those major past conflicts and their educational aftermath. In reaction to these legacies, and in addition to the formal and non-formal initiatives to combat them, such as aid agencies and NGOs, a more focused educational response to the occurrence of disasters has developed, and has come to be known as Education in Emergencies. It relates to both man-made and natural disasters, but human conflict and its implications will be discussed first.

Education in Emergencies is an emergent field of activity that has developed rapidly over the past two decades or so. That is why it was appropriate to precede discussion of it by the more fundamental relationship between war and education. Not only has that relationship been evident for centuries, the timescale of a full war, which necessarily involves international dimensions, tends to be a long one. However, there are always overlaps. Some wars are very brief, as was the so-called 'Gulf War' of 1991, while other wars, such as the one in Afghanistan, though they may be attenuated, began after Education in Emergencies became an active field, with the result that international reconstructive efforts in education and other areas are in progress concomitantly with the war. As Table 4.2 shows, Afghanistan is a major recipient of aid, a proportion of it going to support education at various levels, including some dedicated support for learning opportunities for women and girls. Nonetheless, the majority of humanitarian educational work in the conventional sense is related to what is termed 'conflict' and 'post-conflict' situations on a smaller scale.

The literature relating to education in, and in response to, situations of conflict and post-conflict has grown more rapidly and more substantially since the turn of the millennium than that relating to natural disasters, or to the needs of the marginalized majority. There may be a number of reasons for this. The depths of the crises are more immediately evident as the number of countries with violent conflict issues grows. This is the reason why the 2011 GMR is to be dedicated to this theme. To some degree this has been stimulated by the pioneer work of Brendan O'Malley on *Education Under Attack*, first published by UNESCO in 2007, and again in a thoroughly revised and expanded form in 2010 (UNESCO, 2010a). O'Malley's work is very specific in that it concentrates on direct and violent assaults on teachers and other educators, as well as on the physical fabric of schools. A very appropriate associated volume, in the sense of a humanitarian response, also published by UNESCO in 2010, is *Protecting Education from Attack* (UNESCO, 2010b). The attacks described and analysed in these studies are sometimes part of a broader conflict such as a civil war and sometimes separate, so more reference will be made to them later, but they are highlighted here because their specificity and detail attracts attention and concentrates the mind.

Another branch of UNESCO, the International Bureau of Education (IBE) in Geneva, published an important volume in 2004, *Education, Conflict and Social Cohesion*, edited by Sobhi Tawil and Alexandra Harley, in which an attempt was made to classify conflicts – defined as violent armed conflicts – in different ways. They recognized: 'troubles', as in Northern Ireland and South Africa; military coups, as in Chile in 1973; civil war, as in Lebanon; separatist armed struggle, as in Sierra Leone; and genocide/ethnic cleansing, as in Rwanda and Bosnia. As ever with attempted classifications, there are 'grey areas'. The Sierra Leone conflict throughout the 1990s was, and is, normally referred to as a civil war, but in fact was not as clear-cut as that. In all these, and in the many other cases, what happens is very context-specific. As is conventional, Tawil and Harley look at conflict and education in terms of the other end of the spectrum, the achievement of social cohesion at the national level. This makes their attempt to relate conflict status and type of educational initiative, shown as Table 4.3 here, somewhat unreal, though it does make a contribution to the discourse.

| Conflict status | Non-conflict; relative 'peace' | Internal trouble; social unrest; 'pre'-conflict | Armed conflict | Transition out of violence; peace process | 'Post-' conflict |
|---|---|---|---|---|---|
| Type of initiative | Education for prevention (development) | | Education in Emergencies | Education for social and civic reconstruction (development) | |

*Table 4.3  Conflict status and type of educational initiative*

*Source: IBE, 2004, 11*

Their sequence begins with relative peace and 'education for prevention', which one must assume are regarded as normal and satisfactory situations. While the 'relative' qualification of peace is a realistic description of most societies without violent conflict currently taking place, the idea that what passes for normal uninterrupted formal educational provision is a positive component of such situations is definitely not. This is in fact illustrated by the opening statement of the then director of the IBE, Cecilia Braslavsky, in her preface to the book:

> Conflict has recently emerged as one of the challenges for reaching Education for All goals. International attention, initially concerned with the destructive and disruptive impact of armed conflict on education systems, has now turned to the more subtle and complex relationships between education and conflict. There is a growing international awareness of the potential for educational governance, schooling structures, as well as teaching and learning content and methods to act as catalysts for the outbreak of violent conflict.
>
> (IBE, 2004, v)

This view is very much the starting point for another important publication in this field, that of Lynn Davies (2004), which has had a significant influence on the approach to the notion of education as a humanitarian response being put forward in this book. A very accessible entrée to the arguments put forward by Lynn Davies is her article 'Education in the Twenty-first Century: Conflict, Reconciliation and Reconstruction' (2005). The title is prompted by the rapid increase in situations of conflict, which inevitably affects education. However, the presumable aim of the title to universalize the issue is extremely apt, whether intentional or not. Lynn Davies certainly takes that more fundamental view when she suggests: 'We have a crisis: not of globalisation, not of the economy but of something that transcends those. It is a crisis of the refusal to see what is happening to learning in our societies' (358). She goes on to refer to 'the myth that universal formal education automatically creates international harmony'. The fundamental issue that she observes, and which has been stressed throughout this book, is that education reflects society and not the reverse. This does not mean that education has nothing to offer by way of helping to engender greater social cohesion, but the most telling word in her reference to 'the myth' is 'formal'. There has to be a holistic educational approach, as argued for above and which includes informal and non-formal modes of education as well. Again, this is not because the non-formal and informal are blameless with regard to engendering conflict. In fact, quite the reverse, because they are more influential than the formal in ways ranging from military training, sectarianism in religious teaching and marketization of everyday life to the preponderance of violent action in video games apparently enjoyed by many millions of adults as well as children.

Education in emergencies is making its contribution on two fronts: (1) the intellectual and academic discourse and literature, and (2) practitioner action and training. At best they can be mutually supportive by academics getting involved in field activities and practitioners entering on and/or contributing to programmes in universities. This mutual self-interest is no bad thing, but there is a danger of 'preciousness' taking over if altruism rules, as sometimes it does. The close relationship that now exists between theory and practice in modern methods for the training of doctors, nurses and teachers is a sound example for acquiring the expertise to operate in emergencies. Indeed, because they are emergencies it is often the case that educators, health professionals and engineers will necessarily work together in the immediate response.

One of the most important innovations engendering awareness of appropriate responses to disasters among educators is the Inter-Agency Network for Education in Emergencies (INEE), founded in 2000 as a response to the Dakar meeting called to review progress since Jomtien in 1990. INEE's strength, moral as well as practical, is that it is an open global network of interested individuals numbering nearly 3,000. It refers to itself as 'half-organised', which is not an indication of a degree of chaos but a deliberate decision to enhance innovation, flexibility and a rapid response to emergency situations. Its operational framework in itself illustrates its minimal formal identity and virtual lack of bureaucracy as it operates through four bases:

1. The *International Rescue Committee* in New York, from where the Director operates.
2. The *UNHCR* Division of Operational Services in Geneva.
3. The *UNICEF* Education Sector in New York.
4. The *UNESCO* Section for Education in Post-Conflict and Post-Disaster Situations in Paris.

Table 4.4 illustrates the culture of INEE and its objectives.

---

- A clear shared vision and collective determination to ensure education becomes a priority humanitarian response.

- A motivated and responsive global team of individual members. Steering Group representatives and Secretariat staff working with and for the leading organizations in the field.

- A commitment to collaboration, flexibility, openness and transparency.

- Core funding, resources and in-kind contributions leveraged from and through diverse sources.

- Inclusive and interactive membership communication mechanisms including the listserv, Minimum Standards consultations and training, Task Teams, Interest Groups, and French, Spanish and Portuguese Communities.

- A strategic approach which harnesses the power of a global network to consultatively determine priorities and respond to the dynamic nature of the field.

---

*Table 4.4 The Culture of Inter-agency Network for Education in Emergencies (INEE)*

*Source: INEE*

The fact that the section of UNESCO in Paris within which part of INEE is lodged is in the Division for Educational Strategies and Capacity Building is potentially very significant. As has been discussed above, capacity-building, especially with regard to cultural capacity, is fundamental to addressing the dysfunctionality of education evident to a greater or lesser extent in all countries. That is what makes education a global concern. One of the concerns about the model reproduced as Table 4.3 above is its implied acceptance of the national paradigm and its outcome from the emergency, transitional and post-conflict phases as being social and civic reconstruction rather than reform. To some extent, this brings us back to the dilemma as to what constitutes an emergency. Disasters have tended to occur post-1945 much more in the world of the marginalized majority than that of the disparate and dysfunctional mainstream. Their, in general, smaller temporal and spatial scales than those that applied to past major, sometimes global, conflicts have led to the use of the term 'emergency' with all that it implies. INEE is already into its second decade, and the events to which it is responding are growing in number and longevity. The conflicts in Myanmar, Sudan, Congo Republic and Colombia are just four seemingly intractable examples with decades under their belt. For Palestinians the timescale is at least seventy years.

As Alan Smith (2005) reports, research would indicate that a number of global trends are informing a changing context for education in the twenty-first century which will be increasingly challenging. The trends and predictions he outlines are (373–4):

1　The economic gap between countries will widen significantly, poverty will increase.
2　Information technologies will dramatically reduce the privacy of individuals.
3　Inequalities between those who have access to information technologies and those who do not will increase dramatically.
4　The cost of obtaining adequate water will increase due to population growth.
5　Deforestation and environmental deterioration.
6　Conflict of interest between developed and developing countries will increase.
7　Migration flows from poor to rich areas within and between countries will have an impact on security and social order.
8　Increased use of genetic engineering will create more complex ethical questions.
9　Economic growth will be fuelled by knowledge, ideas and innovations more than by natural resources.

Some of these issues clearly illustrate the overlap between human conflict and natural disasters. Others imply, rightly, that the escalating sophistication of modern technology, including ICT, has the capacity to make things worse as well as better. This is clear from contemporary conflicts themselves, where mobile phones and hand-held computers are playing their part even in extremely poor and underdeveloped parts of the world. But it is important, while being realistic about the downsides in education itself, as well as wider global instability, to seek

LIVERPOOL JOHN MOORES UNIVERSITY
LEARNING SERVICES

out the ways in which education could play a more positive role. The first, and fundamental, step along the way is for educators, especially those involved in the academic field of educational studies, to recognize and accept the reality of the limitations and shortcomings of formal education. As Susan Nicolai (2009) puts it: 'Despite the clear importance of the broader political and socio-economic context, understanding of education reform has tended to be limited to its focus on educational aspects without considering the broader role in societal reform' (47–8). This takes us back to the point made in Chapter 1 that the education profession, especially at tertiary level, is extraordinarily conservative and virtually blind to the imperative of routine involvement with the non-formal and especially informal modes if the potentially beneficial contribution of education to human well-being is to be realized.

Lyndsay Bird (2006) emphasizes this issue. Focusing on the opportunities for innovation that inevitably arise in situations of conflict, she observes:

> NGOs and civil society groups – being close to the areas of conflict – become aware of and therefore take advantage of opportunities for innovation that arise during conflict. These may include new curricula, methods of teaching or home-based learning. NGOs, state authorities and donors supporting post-conflict reconstruction need to capture small-scale innovations and to scale up or mainstream them without losing the freshness and direct approach that give them an innovative edge. We need to ask if the current funding modalities of post-conflict reconstruction – focusing on sector or budget support rather than projects – provide less opportunity for innovation? Should donors set aside funds for innovation and directly support the scaling-up of innovative approaches? How can academic research institutions be encouraged to support such innovation?
>
> A disconnect still exists – despite the best efforts of events such as the University of Oxford and UNICEF Education and Conflict Conference – between the field and the research communities. There is a need to build on work already being done by some NGOs/agencies to build a research component into country programmes and/or to establish linkages between academic institutions and field-level NGO staff in order to support in-country research, document lessons learned and more wisely disseminate best practice.
>
> (Bird, 2006, 30)

Some might think this a rather harsh critique of the academic side, especially with clearly significant contributions from scholars such as Bob Moon, Lynn Davies and Alan Smith cited above. The fact is that with educational studies itself being marginalized in many universities, and concentrating its efforts on the formal dimension of learning, where the majority of research-funding possibilities reside, those concerned with fields such as comparative education and international educational development find themselves on the periphery of the periphery. Another problem is that of structural and bureaucratic rigidities such as were evident in the 1980s in England when the 'recent and relevant' imperative required teacher trainers to return to the classroom full-time. Ideally, this should have been for more than one term and in exchange with a schoolteacher, but the complications of different budget lines and pension regulations acted against this. To achieve what Lyndsay Bird rightly advocates, academics would need to spend lengthy periods of time in the field, that is to say a minimum of six months each time, for them to play a meaningful research role alongside practitioners. The implications for their teaching and examining roles in their institutions would have to be resolved. Perhaps this could be achieved by the temporary re-employment of retired academics in this field, much as with the retired headteachers in Sierra Leone mentioned above, making use of the key role they could have played in teacher education had the civil war not prevented it. This would release younger academics to go into the field without detriment to ongoing teaching at their home universities. The cost implications of this on any significant scale, especially at a time of public spending austerity, would seem to be prohibitive.

As it stands, in any case we have very important research contributions not only from practitioners such as Susan Nicolai but also from agency advisers such as Peter Colenso of DfID and Peter Buckland of the World Bank. The latter is the author of the most authoritative survey of responses to education and conflict in the early twenty-first century, *Reshaping the Future: Education and Post-Conflict Re-construction* (2005). In a 2006 article, Peter Buckland encapsulated his argument in two sets of statements: 'problems common to many post-conflict states' and 'the way ahead'.

These have been brought together here as Table 4.5.

| Problems common to many post-conflict states | The way ahead |
|---|---|
| Inability of recovering states to fund either capital or recurrent expenditure | Early focus on getting schools functioning so that the return of young people to classes can be seen as a 'peace dividend' and shore up support for peace |
| Chronic shortages of qualified teachers – many have been killed or have fled, and many of those who remain or return take work for international agencies or NGOs | |
| Oversupply of under-qualified or unqualified teachers | Bold symbolic actions (such as purging inflammatory textbooks) to signal that, while much about the system remains unchanged, reform has started |
| The sheer numbers of war-affected youth, demobilized soldiers and young people who have not completed basic education | |
| Poor record-keeping, corruption and lack of transparency in education governance: salaries are often paid to 'ghost' teachers | Decentralization reforms to allow parents space to be involved in school governance |
| The 'relief bubble' in international financial support often subsides before a more predictable flow of reconstruction resources can be mobilized: relief agencies often scale back operations before development-focused agencies can be mobilized | Acknowledgement that creating an equitable system able to deliver quality education is an incremental and ongoing process that takes decades and will require national consensus around a wider development vision of where a country is heading |
| Skills training for youth is seriously under-sourced: even when available, vocational training programmes often fail to prepare people for locally available employment opportunities | Capacity-building, encouragement of participation and coordination between communities, teachers and their organizations, local authorities and other stakeholders |
| Coordination challenges: as education involves an interface of humanitarian action and development in complex ways there is often a plethora of coordination mechanisms | Recognition that returning refugees, and especially youth, can contribute to the process of education reconstruction |
| Failure to develop successful initiatives to build the skills of young people and prevent their recruitment into military or criminal activity: youth are seen as a threat to stability and few programmes value young people as an important resource for development and reconstruction | Ensuring that external support for education builds on – and does not compete with – the efforts of local communities and authorities already active in supporting education |

*Table 4.5  Peter Buckland's post-conflict education reality check*

Source: Buckland, 2006, 7–8

Because disasters and emergencies are contexts where integration of the modes of education is unavoidable, the holistic nature of humanitarian responses is an indication of what is also needed in the wider contexts of the marginalized majority and the dysfunctional mainstream. Susan Nicolai concludes her general review and critique of the situation of education in emergencies with a summary of lessons learnt from the case studies that comprise the remainder of her book. They are listed as Table 4.6.

---

- Long-term investment is an important past of achieving major and sustained education gains during and following crises.

- An early and coordinated focus on capacity-building should underpin education system development in conflict-affected states.

- Education innovation can boost access and quality objectives significantly, provided they include appropriate efforts towards alignment and scale-up.

- A focus on teachers, both in terms of training and conditions, is an essential area of support due to teachers' pivotal role in education delivery.

- Investment in a curriculum and textbook development or renewal is a major opportunity for change that links closely with broader government aims following conflict.

- Efforts towards conflict prevention and peace-building should be infused across education interventions during and following a conflict.

- The protection and security of students and teachers, along with that of the broader community and of aid workers, should be actively pursued in all conflict and recovery situations.

- Strong partnerships, in their myriad forms, serve as a foundation for a positive education change in conflict and recovery contexts.

---

*Table 4.6 Susan Nicolai's lessons learned for education from conflict situations*

Source: Nicolai, 2009

While Peter Buckland's recommendations are more specific to conflict and post-conflict situations than others, Susan Nicolai's would seem to have the potential to be applied to emergencies arising from natural disasters as well as to the majority of dysfunctional mainstream systems.

In the previous chapter on the marginalized majority, a number of human groups were identified as being in particular need of a more humanitarian approach to meeting their educational needs, notably orphans and vulnerable children (OVCs), indigenous peoples and travelling communities. These groups could well be affected by violent conflict (as indeed has a prime example, the Roma people), but their existence on the margins is not primarily to do with that. The majority of OVCs owe their plight more to other socio-economic and political factors such as extreme poverty, neglect, criminality and wilful exclusion. The issue of minorities within mainstream societies and education systems will be addressed later, but two groups that also appear within those systems but are the products of conflict or violent oppression are refugees and internally displaced people.

# Refugees and asylum seekers

Refugees and asylum seekers are a very special category of the world's human population not only because of their massive, and ever-increasing, numbers but also because of their presence in virtually every country. Some countries, for example Yemen, are significant sources of refugees as well as being host countries for refugees from elsewhere. The definition of the term 'refugee' varies considerably from that given in the United Nations convention to however individual countries choose to define it in practice. Refugees were defined as a legal group following the massive numbers fleeing Europe during and after the 1939–45 world war. The UN, founded in 1945, set up a Convention Relating to the Status of Refugees which, from 1951, was

> A refugee is a person who (according to the formal definition of 1A of this (1951) Convention), owing to a well founded fear of being persecuted on account of race, nationality, membership of a particular social group, or political opinion, is outside of their nationality, and is unable to or, owing to such fear, is unwilling to avail him/herself of the protection of that country.

The UN Protocol was expanded in 1967, and by regional protocols in Africa and Latin America, to include persons who had fled war or other violence in their home country.

For obvious reasons it takes time for the verification of the claims of any such person to be checked and, pending the decision of the receiving country to grant refugee status or not, the person is defined as an asylum seeker. The power lies with the host country, and it may well be the case that full asylum seeker status will not be granted and that instead such designations as 'residential status' or 'illegal alien' may be applied. Each status carries with it different degrees of access (if any at all) to the formal system of education in the host country. It also varies from country to country as to whether refugees, asylum seekers or lesser categories are required to be in camps or permitted to live in the wider society with certain restrictions. For example, the various indigenous minority peoples in eastern Myanmar, such as the Karen and the Kareni, who are being persecuted by the Burmese-dominated regime, when they cross the border into Thailand either choose to be registered as refugees or melt into Thai society as illegal immigrants. Some move through and into Malaysia. Those who register as refugees in Thailand gain the support of the United Nations High Commissioner for Refugees (UNHCR), and are required to live in camps where they receive international support through NGOs for their protection, nutrition, health and education. Those who choose not to register receive no such support either from UNHCR or the Thai government. They may be able to survive in the local rural economy due to the fact that Karen, Kareni and other indigenous people live on either side of the Myanmar/Thailand border because the boundary was drawn through their traditional territories by Britain during the colonial period. As indicated above, the dynamics of political geography are an important factor in conflict and migration.

The situation for the Palestinians is even more complicated, as it dates from the aftermath of the Ottoman Empire and includes the creation of the state of Israel, which has made the Palestinians stateless. Palestinian refugees exist as a diaspora across the world, but especially in neighbouring countries, and both external and internal political geographical parameters are still shifting. They will be mentioned in more detail below, but first the global situation will be outlined.

According to the USA Committee for Refugees, there are over 60 million worldwide, plus about 35 million internally displaced people (IDPs). As indicated above, the UNHCR is the prime international agency for assisting refugees, and in 2010 is dealing with over 20 million of what it terms 'persons of concern'. This comprises refugees (10 million plus), asylum seekers (c. 1 million), returnees (c. 2 million), stateless people (c. 2 million), IDPs (c. 7 million) and 'others' (c. 1 million). The largest concentrations of refugees are not, with the exception of China, in countries with the world's major economies. They are, in broad figures: Iran (c. 1 million from Afghanistan and Iraq); Pakistan (c. 500,000 from Afghanistan); Tanzania (c. 500,000 from Burundi and Congo); Saudi Arabia (c. 500,000 from Palestine; Serbia (c. 300,000 from Bosnia and Croatia); China (c. 300,000 from Vietnam); Thailand (c. 250,000 from Myanmar); and Armenia (c. 200,000 from Azerbaijan). Overall the main concentrations of refugee communities are in Central Africa, East Africa and South-West Asia (the majority of the Middle East). The UNHCR has 260 offices across 116 countries, employing in total over 7,000 staff, most of them in field locations. By far the highest donor is the USA (with over $US300 million), followed by Japan, the European Union and the Netherlands (each about $US80 million); Sweden (c. $US60 million); Norway, Denmark and the UK (each with c. $US50 million); and Germany (c. US$40 million). The geographical concentration of the major donors is striking, with the Netherlands outstanding in relation to its own population size.

In terms of its response, the UNHCR concentrates on what it terms 'durable solutions', which comprise: (1) international protection; (2) repatriation; and (3) resettlement in third countries. At the same time, the agency has to help support those refugees registered with it in key areas of survival and development such as nutrition, health and education. As stated in the 2006 UNHCR Global Appeal:

> In the meantime, a facilitating element of any durable solution is building the capacity of the refugees to attain self-reliance by enhancing their skills and capacities, and providing them with the necessary tools (e.g. loans, land and income-generating projects). Evidence suggests that the most effective means to foster self-reliance within refugee populations is to focus on the circumstances they face and remove the obstacles to their productivity. Consideration also needs to be given to the human and material assets refugees bring with them and how these can be utilized to support development.
>
> (UNHCR, 2006b, 24)

The complexity of refugee situations regarding education can be illustrated by the case of the Karen refugees in Thailand, with which the writer was involved. Those who chose to register as refugees are contained within eight camps along the western border with Myanmar. As already mentioned, many others, under duress from the Burmese-dominated regime in Myanmar, simply crossed the border illegally and have to fend for themselves. The UNHCR has oversight for the refugees in the camps, including their education. Since these are closed camps, the primary and secondary schools are constructed from local materials within, just as are other service buildings and the homes of the families. Teachers have to come from within the camp community, and in any case the curriculum has to be delivered in the Karen language because learning Thai is not permitted. This is partly to discourage the refugees from breaking out into the wider community, but also because the Karen have ownership of the system within the camp through the Karen Education Committee, which has its very modest headquarters in Bangkok. UNHCR, the Thai government, the Karen Committee and a consortium of NGOs in the capital have to work together to try to provide and support different aspects of, mostly formal, education. So there has to be agreement to outsource specific programmes of education support to appropriate NGOs, all of whom set up their own headquarters in the regional centre of Mai Sot, located in the middle of the north–south string of camps along the border. The Netherlands NGO, ZOA, with which the writer worked, was contracted to enhance teacher training within the camps of the Karen. All teachers in the camp schools had, necessarily, to be Karen refugees. A few had enjoyed primary and secondary schooling and a tiny minority had teaching experience. Most teachers had themselves received only primary schooling. The NGO employed mostly local staff to provide teacher training in the camps as well as some research and evaluation from outsiders.

Mention was made above of UNHCR's priorities for durable solutions, such as repatriation, and resettlement to third countries. In this case, repatriation is still hardly an option given the sustained oppression of the Karen by the Burmese-dominated Myanmar government. Not surprisingly, those interested in third-country resettlement are the better educated who can understand and exploit the protracted process of selection by UNHCR and the potential host countries, which include the UK. For their part, the potential hosts are keen to take only those with levels of education and skill that will contribute to their own economies. The result is that the teaching force in the Karen camps is being constantly disrupted and depleted by the departures of its already limited talent, and the NGO is routinely reinventing the wheel as it revolves. The process is a downward spiral, as what comes in is rarely of the quality of what goes out. This applies equally to other NGOs dealing with different aspects of education in the camps. Of those opting for and selected by the UK as a resettlement destination, most Karen have been relocated to Sheffield as part of the policy to help refugees maintain their cultural cohesion.

The case of the Palestinian refugees is even more complicated as their problem has been festering for nearly four times as long as that of those leaving Myanmar, and their experience with regard to educational opportunities in host countries varies sharply from country to country. A Palestinian refugee is uniquely defined, namely as being a person 'whose normal place of residence was Palestine between June 1946 and May 1948 but who lost their home and means of livelihood as a result of the 1948 Arab–Israeli conflict and their descendents, whether they are in refugees camps or not'. A special UN agency was established to support such refugees – the United Nations Relief and Works Agency in the Near East (UNRWA), whose remit excludes all Palestinian refugees who are not in the following territories: Syria, Jordan, Lebanon, the West Bank and Gaza. This totals over 5 million refugees, of whom 1 million are in camps. But the global total of Palestinian refugees much exceeds this number with concentrations in other Middle Eastern and North African (MENA) countries from Saudi Arabia across to Morocco. Indeed, Saudi Arabia recognized the problem as long ago as 1935, and, as indicated above, has over 500,000 Palestinian refugees according to UNHCR, some of whom have come from Iraq as a result of the recent conflict there.

The educational opportunities and experiences of Palestinian refugees vary greatly according to which host country they are in and whether they are in camps or not. For example, in Jordan, Palestinian refugees have long since been granted Jordanian citizenship, and therefore have the same right and access as all other members of the country. Some have risen to high levels in the education sector of that country. In Syria, they also have open access to all opportunities available to the citizens of that country, but by contrast in neighbouring Lebanon, Palestinian refugees are confined to camps and their schooling is provided by the United Nations Relief and Works Agency (UNRWA). However, they cannot gain access to employment or further study in the Lebanese system, and the qualifications they do gain are not recognized outside. The very longstanding nature of these camps creates unique, almost indigenous, societies – worlds of their own. So much so that when one of the major camps in Lebanon was destroyed by conflict, the scattered remnants of the camp society were unable to adjust to unexpected access to schools and other services. They became instead a cultural network clinging together with the help of humanitarian agencies. In so doing, their relationship to the mainstream was very similar to that of travelling communities and indigenous peoples.

Some Palestinians have the extraordinary experience of being in a refugee camp within their own territory, i.e. in the West Bank or Gaza, because technically they have no country and are officially stateless. The quasi-national governments of the Palestinian Territory – politically estranged between Gaza and the West Bank – provide schooling with the help of outside support, while the several Palestinian universities are privately run. Overall, the educational standard amongst Palestinians, with the exception of those in the closed camps, is the highest in the Arab world. Nonetheless, the fate of the Palestinians is tragic. Their educational achievements and frustrations cannot be comprehended without taking into account the temporal and spatial scales of examination referred to above, from the Ottoman legacy of the 1920s to the effect on school access of the internal walls built across their land by Israel nearly a century later. This very special case can be followed up by recourse to Susan Nicolai's outstanding book *Fragmented Foundations: Education and Chronic Crisis in the Occupied Palestinian Territory* (2007).

As far as the UK is concerned, there are many NGOs attending to the educational needs of refugees. Although the main NGO concerned with education, the Refugee Council, has a much wider remit for the well-being of refugees, it pays a great deal of attention to schooling. Based in London, where the majority of UK refugees are located, it interacts with the education services of all the London boroughs. Each has its dedicated officers for refugee education, especially schooling, who are at the interface between the schools and the existing hierarchy of regulations. Being in the European Union, the UK is subject to regulations at that level. Then there are national regulations and guidelines that vary across the UK due to the devolved powers of its constituent parts, and finally each local authority has its own guidelines. Because of this bureaucratic nightmare and the urgent and fundamental needs of refugees, it falls to headteachers to use their discretion, which in most cases means that they admit the children immediately. Not only does this relate positively to the international rights of the children, it also frees up refugee parents to solve other urgent problems and perhaps even to gain meaningful employment. A somewhat similar situation obtains regarding travelling communities, for whom some local authorities have dedicated staff, such is the demand. At the school and local level the needs of the refugees come first. When former secretary of state for education, David Blunkett, proposed to set up camps for refugees and asylum seekers in England, including schools, this was met with immediate protest from headteachers, who pointed out that they, their staff and existing pupils greatly valued the intercultural dimension refugee children and families brought to their schools. The plan was dropped.

As far as further and higher education is concerned, the NGO World University Service (WUS) UK has long played a prominent part in supporting refugee students and academics, placing them on appropriate courses in British universities and also assisting with preparing for a return, where possible, to their countries of origin. Such highly educated and skilled men and women represent a vital human resource and are often among the first targets of violent conflict, as has already been pointed out. The potential of this resource may later be realized in the reconstruction in their countries of origin or in resettlement in the host country, as was the case with Ralph Miliband, for instance, who became a leading professor of political science in England and whose two sons became cabinet ministers in the UK government.

# Internally displaced people (IDPs)

Human displacement takes a number of forms. Becoming an asylum seeker, then a refugee is the most obvious and well known. It involves crossing an international border and seeking the recognition and protection of the host country. There are numerous international agreements and conventions regarding refugees, but there may well be as many if not more internally displaced people (IDPs) in the world. According to the 1951 UN Convention, a refugee is a:

> person who, owing to a well-founded fear of being persecuted for reasons of race, religion, nationality, membership of a particular social group or political opinion, is outside the country of his nationality, and is unable or, owing to such fear, unwilling to avail himself of the protection of that country.
>
> (UNHCR, 2006b, 13 ).

In the same way that UNHCR can support only a small proportion of the world's refugees, it can only cater for about 5.5 million of the estimated 25 million IDPs. Even then, education is only one of a range of services it provides. Before mentioning some of the major examples of obvious IDPs, it is necessary to recognize examples of conditions arising from, or related to, conflict that have produced anomalous situations.

It is evident from the Palestinian case that in addition to generating a massive number of refugees, it also exhibits the issue of internal displacement. However, it does so in a very unusual way through the creation of a foreign state (Israel) on its territory, with international agreement and support, then the extension of that state by further conquest, then the construction of Jewish settlements on Palestinian land and finally the building of barriers through community localities. Technically, Palestine is not yet a state but a territory. This highly idiosyncratic case can be followed up by recourse to: (1) Nicolai (2007); (2) Brock and Demirdjian (2010); and (3) Plonski (2005).

The Palestinian case involves a considerable number of 'returnees', a category with somewhat different experiences and needs from those who have remained, albeit displaced, within their homeland. Returnees are not necessarily welcomed by those who have suffered external oppression at home often over a significant length of time. This applied to those Namibians who fled from South African oppression to Zimbabwe and expected to have key roles in their liberated state when they returned, having had the support, including educational, of the international community. Somalia is a country long wrought with internal strife, and in 1991 the north-west region declared itself to be the Independent Republic of Somaliland. It is, however, not recognized by the United Nations and therefore receives very little support from multilateral and bilateral international development agencies. Despite this, UNICEF has given assistance, as have a range of NGOs. So the people of Somaliland are displaced by virtue of a change of political geography, not their own migration.

Another anomalous case is Diego Garcia, once an atoll colony of the UK in the Indian Ocean, part of the Chagos Archipelago. This is a complicated story told succinctly by John Pilger (2006). Briefly, the Chagos Archipelago had been a British colony since 1815 and by 1964 had a population of some 2,000, descendants of a slave population working coconut plantations. In that year, a secret deal was agreed between the UK and the USA, which wanted a location in the Indian Ocean for a military air base from which to operate over the Middle East and East Asia. A condition of the agreement was that there should be no local population and so the UK government forcibly removed the inhabitants to Mauritius in a deal with the government there, which gave them no support, educational or otherwise. Another unusual example is the case of the 'Pakistanis' of Bangladesh who number about 200,000. They were left stranded when Pakistan, founded in 1947 on the partition of British India, split into two in 1971, an Urdu-speaking west and a Bangla-speaking east that became the independent country of Bangladesh. Some sixty years later, this enclave of Urdu speakers subsist in sixty-six camps, the rump of a cultural group most of which did manage to get to Pakistan. They receive no educational support from either Bangladesh or Pakistan.

There are other anomalous situations around the world, but we need to turn now to the major examples of internally displaced populations. Reference has been made to the Karen and Kareni refugees from Myanmar who live in UNHCR camps across the border in Thailand. They, and those who spill over into Thailand as illegal economic migrants, are just a small proportion of those affected within Myanmar by two types of displacement known as 'conflict induced' and 'development induced'. The former involves military takeover, the latter involve the takeover of traditional land for so-called national development schemes. Well over a million people have been displaced. Children are targeted for the military, and schools destroyed, as are attempts at non-formal education within communities. As in many examples of large-scale internal displacement, international humanitarian agencies and NGOs are severely restricted in what they are permitted to do. The priorities are shelter, safety, food and health. Figure 4.1 shows the main areas of internal displacement within Myanmar near the Thai border.

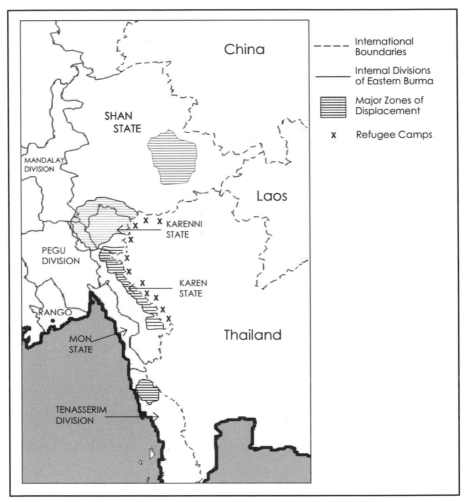

*Figure 4.1 Internal displacement in Eastern Burma*

Sudan is a country which features several forms of displacement. The best known is in the Darfur region to the west of the country, bordering on Chad. At its peak there were over 2 million IDPs in Darfur, of which about 650,000 in West Darfur were surviving under the aegis of UNHCR. Though still volatile, the situation has eased, with some IDPs returning to their localities, but this has been more than matched by the large number of returnees from Chad. Much of the effort of UNHCR in this region has had to be concentrated on protection, survival and health support, but it has to be appreciated that these all carry with them important elements of non-formal and informal education. Special efforts have been directed towards the support and education of women, who have suffered disproportionately. These include the provision of safe spaces for women, where they can help each other through informal discussion and learn to deal with sexual and gender-based violence (known as SGBV). They also learn to use fuel-efficient stoves, help run youth centres and disseminate what they have acquired regarding health education, especially in respect of HIV/AIDS. All this will help to encourage modest developments in the learning cultures of communities if and when they gain sufficient security and confidence to settle again. Some of Darfur's IDPs are nomadic, with attitudes to formal education similar to those mentioned above with regard to the Rabaris of Kutch in India and other travelling peoples. Here it is best to help by protecting and re-establishing their traditional grazing cycles and movements in relation to which their informal traditional education is endemic and self-contained. This is particularly difficult as both conflict and mass migration have often enhanced the degradation of the natural environment to the point of desertification.

In addition to Darfur, Sudan exhibits a complicated picture of displacement in its eastern and southern areas. It is both the recipient and provider of refugees with regard to its neighbours Eritrea, Ethiopia, Kenya, Uganda and the Democratic Republic of Congo, and in and from those border regions there are considerable numbers of IDPs. Many conflicts lie behind these disasters, some going back centuries. The educational outcome of more recent conflict in the south was aptly encapsulated by Marc Sommers (2005) as 'islands of education within oceans of destruction'. One of the most telling parts of his report is on the issue of IDPs in the country's capital, Khartoum. The bare facts, as far as we have them, are extraordinary. He writes, bearing in mind that the Sudan government does not officially distinguish between IDPs and others: 'The National Population Council and the United Nations have jointly estimated that out of 4.4 million residents in Khartoum, fully 1.8 million – 41 per cent – are IDPs' (207). With only a tiny fraction living in organized camps, the vast majority occupy massive squatter settlements, which from time to time are destroyed by the authorities and then re-emerge. Among the elements of a primitive infrastructure in the squatter settlements are schools, which are destroyed along with all else. Figure 4.2 illustrates both the peripheral and the centrifugal forces of displacement faced by Sudan, one of the poorest countries in the world and Africa's largest nation in area.

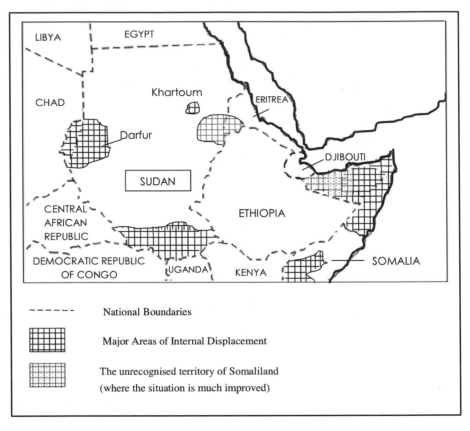

*Figure 4.2 Areas of displacement in East and the Horn of Africa*

Colombia is second only to Sudan in terms of IDPs but for very different reasons. For decades an extensive internal armed conflict has been raging between government forces, paramilitary groups and guerrillas. This is not a civil war in the conventional sense, but a widespread conflict relating to drugs that, as the UNHCR puts it, 'continues to impinge on the enjoyment of basic human rights by the civilian population, and leaves whole communities at risk of displacement'. Estimates of the number of IDPs range between 2 to 3 million, and there are thousands of Colombian refugees in some neighbouring countries. As already mentioned, all forms of education can contribute to the generation of conflict, but in Colombia the situation is largely the reverse. The aforementioned 2010 new edition of *Education Under Attack*, published by UNESCO reports that over the decade beginning in 1999, nearly 400 teachers had been murdered and many more tortured, threatened or forced to leave their schools. Many schools have been destroyed and universities infiltrated and attacked in violent conflict that is not just indiscriminate but targeted. The report goes on to give details of attacks on schools, colleges, universities, their students, teachers and others involved in education, such as aid workers, in thirty-two countries. In all of these cases, and in over twenty more that will be added in the 2011 GMR on conflict and education, a great deal of internal displacement is involved that is almost impossible to quantify. This makes the estimate of 25 million IDPs in the world likely to be a gross undercalculation.

# Education and environmental disasters

At first sight, there might seem to be a clear distinction between problems for education arising from conflict situations and those arising from so-called 'natural disasters'. In reality, there are many overlaps in causes and consequences as well as in humanitarian responses, and both exhibit extremes of temporal scale from centuries to seconds. Just as the macro picture of the relationship between wars and education was a necessary backdrop to more specific contemporary issues, a discussion of the broader relationship between human populations and their environment is pertinent here, which is why the term 'environmental disasters' is preferred.

The year 2010 was designated as the International Year of Biodiversity and contained three major events: the launch of the Third Global Biodiversity Outlook (GBO-3) in Nairobi; an independent scientific review to be presented to the UN General Assembly in September 2010; and the Nagoya Biodiversity Summit in October 2010. This will prepare the way for the Rio + 20 Biodiversity Conference in 2012. What have these events to do with education and environmental disasters? After all, human beings were not responsible for the Indian Ocean tsunami of 2004 or the Haiti earthquake of 2010. They are important because they will help to enhance the likelihood of disaster risk reduction, as well as appropriate humanitarian responses to future disasters, provided that the development of education in all its forms takes their findings into account. This will depend on structural, financial and curricular reforms that enable and utilize links between formal, non-formal and informal education to help societies move towards the type of sustainable development appropriate to their changing circumstances. This will necessarily involve interdependent development.

The GBO-3 found that not a single nation had reached its biodiversity targets for 2010, and warned that: 'Natural systems that support economies, lives and livelihoods across the planet are at risk of rapid degradation and collapse unless there is a swift, radical and creative action to conserve and sustainably use the variety of life on Earth.' That reaction can only be impeded by the political stranglehold on education that exists almost everywhere. The report goes on to state that: 'several "tipping points" are approaching in which ecosystems shift to alternative, less productive, states from which it may be difficult or impossible to recover'. It would certainly be inhumane not to react swiftly and positively to the intermittent but frequent environmental disasters that will always occur, such as earthquakes, tsunamis, floods, mudslides, twisters and wildfires. But it is also inhumane to act in such a way as to create the 'dieback' of the Amazon rainforest, or fail to deal with the shift of freshwater lakes, or cause the multiple collapse of coral reef systems, all of which are occurring at an alarming rate. In any case, biodiversity is directly connected with fundamental societal concerns such as poverty reduction, prevention of major diseases and sustainable development. Leaving consideration of such vital issues only in the technical sphere of the highest parts of tertiary education is not good enough. While research at that level is vital, its messages need to be transmitted rapidly down to the local level through all three forms of education.

A good example of the realization of that need and a response to it is the recent work of the geographer Cathrine Brun (2009) of the Norwegian University of Science and technology, Trondheim. She explores the role of researchers in the aftermath of the 2004 Indian Ocean tsunami in Sri Lanka, which she and others later thought to be too detached from the humanitarian responses. She is concerned about the spatial politics of humanitarian work whereby: 'Western politics draws humanitarianism closer to itself while the distance from the people in need seems to increase.' Thus there is a need 'to decolonise humanitarian practice'. The problem to which she refers is very evident when a disaster occurs. Aid agencies, whether multilateral, bilateral or NGOs, seem to find collaboration and coordination difficult, and each wants to publicize its own involvement to the media. At the same time, their individual efforts on the ground are tireless and selfless on behalf of the victims of the disaster. Such a situation became readily apparent in the responses to the Haitian earthquake disaster of 2010. When it comes to the essential research dimension, Cathrine Brun expresses even greater unease, and seeks what she refers to as 'responsible research', by which she means 'research and theories that are meaningful for the research subjects and co-constructed with them' (2009, 201). The approach she advocates to achieve this level of responsibility is 'participatory action research' (PAR), which she describes as:

> a method and field of research aiming at transformation, and [which] can be described as a 'change methodology' because it is about tackling and changing or improving the places within which many

of us practice by promoting collaboration between researchers and local stakeholders. PAR, in this understanding is a decolonising project of particular relevance for those communities whose voices have been silenced, excluded, obscured or otherwise censored.

(Brun, 2009, 204)

It is through such an approach that the essential convergence between the forms of education in the context of reconstruction might be achieved and thus release the latent potential of education to contribute to the essential enhancement of cultural capacity that is fundamental to sustainable development. The underlying principle of PAR is similar to that of participatory rural appraisal in the mainstream development field, but the disaster situation provides the space and the opportunity. What is learnt from such a response could also transfer to the educational context of communities and societies in the worlds of the marginalized majority and the disparate and dysfunctional mainstream.

What is a so-called natural disaster, and what is not, is not always clear-cut. Conflicts, especially those of some length of time, often create or contribute to environmental degradation. With respect to East Africa especially, the Cambridge geographer A.T. Grove pointed this out more than half a century ago in his research illuminating the links between sustained conflict and desertification.

While man-made disasters are almost entirely thought of in terms of war and other dimensions of violent conflict, they can emanate from other activities as in the case of the 2010 BP oil spillage in the Gulf of Mexico, the Bhopal chemical plant explosion in Madhya Pradesh, India in 1984, and the Chernobyl nuclear meltdown crisis near Pripyat in the then USSR in 1986. The Bhopal disaster caused more than half a million people to be exposed to the effects of toxic gases and chemicals. At least 5,000 people were killed; estimates range as high as 25,000. Hundreds of thousands of others were severely affected, with genetic disorders passing through subsequent generations. The legal battle over responsibility and compensation is only now, at the time of writing in June 2010, approaching resolution. As a result of Chernobyl only fifty people were directly killed, but at least 4,000 subsequent cancer deaths have occurred. About 350,000 people were displaced. Although the Chernobyl nuclear plant was located in the former Ukrainian SSR, now independent Ukraine, much of the effects were felt in what is now neighbouring Belarus, and at a lower level across much of Europe.

There have been many other man-made disasters with both ecological and human health effects, and health in itself is an area of major concern that attracts the attention and action of education in emergencies.

# Major nutrition and health issues and education

HIV/AIDS has received the majority of attention since it became apparent about a quarter of a century ago, and it will receive special attention below. But it is important to remember that there are a number of other major debilitating and life-threatening diseases that have been largely eradicated in the developed countries but are still rampant in the world of the marginalized majority.

Health is also connected with disasters, especially of the long-term environmental kind, and is not just a matter of disease. People become susceptible to major and chronic conditions when they are undernourished and overworked as the majority in developing countries are. Hunger and malnutrition are key factors, and although from time to time they receive massive media coverage and welcome relief as a result, the situation in global terms is steadily worsening. It will not only make things worse in the poorest communities in the world, it will affect us all. In October 2009, an Oxfam International report by Alex Renton indicated the wide range of factors at work. It is predicted that: 'The world is going to get hungrier this century, and on a scale that will make the famines of the 1980s look paltry.' This is due to a combination of rapid population increase to an estimated global total of 9.2 billion people by 2050, which is a third more than today's total. The Food and Agriculture Organization (FAO) of the United Nations estimates that to feed that total will require the production of twice as much food as now. Perversely, part of the problem will be caused by the fact that a significant number of people in the developing world will have become richer to the extent that dietary habits will change to be closer to those of the richer nations. The report puts it this way: 'Generally the poor eat vegetables while the rich eat food that eats vegetables. To produce 1 kg of beef takes 10 kg of grass or soya-based food.' It goes on to quote the then British government's chief scientific adviser, John Beddington, saying: 'Food security represents a greater threat to mankind than climate change itself.'

Yet climate change is working in a way that further disadvantages the world's poor majority because the tropical world will get hotter and drier while the cool temperate world will see a more modest temperature increase accompanied by more rain. In any case, for geological reasons, the soils of the temperate world are more fertile than those of the tropical world. This will enable the extension of growing seasons in areas expected to benefit most, such as northern Europe, Canada and northern China. In the intermediate areas of the warm temperate zone such as California and the Mediterranean world, environmental quality will likely deteriorate, and food security with it. Global warming, whatever the reasons for it, is happening, with the resulting rise in sea levels. Some of the most densely populated parts of Asia are coastal, especially estuarine and delta areas. Most are dependent on rice as a staple diet, but the incursion of salt water on the scale that will occur will put an end to any possibility of growing it.

That is for the medium-term future, but the increase in drought and related famine is already evident. In the most severely affected areas such as East Africa, humanitarian responses combine health checks, emergency feeding schemes and non-formal education for adults, mainly mothers. As the health-care NGO Médecins Sans Frontières (MSF) points out in its publicity, in West and East Africa millions of children will die under the age of five. Food is needed during seasonal lean periods, the timing of which used to be understood and prepared for in the traditional indigenous education of the community. Now such periods are unpredictable and often protracted, so at the emergency feeding centres, after the medical check, they may be given what MSF calls 'ready to use foods, milk and peanut-based pastes that do not need to be kept in a refrigerator'. Such pastes, invented and manufactured in France, need to be taken to communities as well, rather than depend on many miles of walking to the health and nutrition centres.

MSF, working in more than sixty countries, highlights the wide range of health situations that exist: for example, high levels of malaria and HIV/AIDS (over half a million) in Burma, both made worse by the neglect and obstruction of the military junta; intensification of diseases in the *barrios* of Colombia where more and more displaced people congregate for safety; high levels of psychosomatic conditions in Chechnya induced by bombing; the almost total collapse of a well-developed system of health care in Zimbabwe, where HIV/AIDS cases have increased dramatically and starvation threatens many; rampant cholera in the Democratic Republic of Congo (DRC) in the midst of rising levels of HIV/AIDS and other conflict-related conditions. They stress the need for greater visibility of severe health problems in all developing countries, pointing out that some, such as the Central African Republic (CAR), are 'starved of attention', becoming 'phantom states'. Yet the CAR and the DRC are supposed to be places of relative safety for displaced people from Sudan.

In addition to the major killers, malaria and cholera, tuberculosis (TB) is still rampant. There has been no significant advance in the treatment of TB for over sixty years. Some late-nineteenth-century treatments are still evident in places. Even worse, only about 50 per cent of TB cases are detected. Uzbekistan is a major case, with over half a million victims. SARS, avian flu and swine flu have all been potential global pandemics in recent years as well. As in so many other environmental situations, our containment of events is far from secure, and education at all levels needs to be more effective in terms of raising awareness of prevention measures everywhere and the support that is needed in the poorest communities.

Although the major diseases mentioned above – malaria, cholera and TB – are the major killers in absolute terms, the condition of HIV/AIDS is a very special one that has rightly attracted a great deal of attention over the few decades since it first appeared. The relatively intense focus on HIV/AIDS is partly because its effect on the younger generations of populations, where it is most prevalent, is so acute and dramatic. Another reason may be that, unlike malaria, TB and cholera, it is a significant problem even in the most highly developed countries of Europe and North America. HIV/AIDS has become one of a small number of UN Priority Areas to be dealt with in the next decade, and is the only disease to have its own designated millennium development goal (MDG 6). One of the main reasons for this is its rapid spread through generations, exacerbating the incidence of malnutrition, poverty, stigmatization and gender disparity. Life-expectancy in the main regions of HIV/AIDS incidence, much of sub-Saharan Africa, has declined to fifty years, and even forty in the worst cases. All this has massive implications for making even a small step towards sustainable development. UNICEF has estimated that globally one in six of AIDS-related deaths are children under the age of five, while in sub-Saharan Africa 85 per cent of such deaths are of people under the age of fifteen. In some locations, it is difficult to ascertain the situation. Examples are the massive and congested shanty towns of Latin America, where much that goes on is concealed, and in the countries of the Middle East and North Africa (MENA), where it is a cultural taboo. But in all parts of the developing world, and especially in sub-Saharan Africa where over two-thirds of HIV/AIDS sufferers are located, the priorities of humanitarian efforts in health and education are, in order: (1) prevention of HIV/AIDS transmission in mothers-to-be; (2) treatment of child victims; (3) prevention among adolescents and young adults; (4) general and adult protection.

The education of girls with regard to HIV/AIDS is crucial. In Africa 75 per cent of the infected are females between fifteen and twenty-five, according to an ActionAid study of 2006, in which it states that progress with education in respect of this disease is being made. Nonetheless, the report admits that: 'The AIDS epidemic continues to evolve, staying one step ahead of our attempts to prevent it' (Hargreaves and Boler, 2006, 3). It is a direct result of gender inequality and needs even greater development in the education of girls to enhance their empowerment to control their own lives. ActionAid advocates the abolition of school fees to enable parents to overcome the opportunity cost of sending their daughters to school. They point out, however, that this will incur a double cost for the governments of the poor countries involved: that is, the reduced income from fees and the increased expenditure on additional students.

This type of issue may relate to the findings of research on spending by developing country governments on health reported in 2010. Academics from the universities of Washington, Seattle and Harvard analysed the records of the WHO and the IMF and published their findings in *The Lancet* on 3 April 2010 (Bhutta et al.). While acknowledging the poor quality of the data recorded to the two international agencies by some governments, they came to the conclusion that governments in developing countries cut the budgets of their health ministries because they were receiving international aid. This does not mean that overall spending on health decreased – in fact the opposite occurred – but that it could have been greater.

## Summary

This chapter on education and disasters and the related issue of education in emergencies has ranged across a quartet of situations that are represented in Table 4.7 as: conflict and post-conflict; natural and 'man'-made disasters; medical and health-related problems; and endemic poverty. The matrix places these against the situations of: inclusion, marginalization and exclusion.

The matrix includes developed as well as developing country examples, in line with the underlying theme of this narrative that education as a humanitarian response should apply everywhere and not just in disaster or emergency situations.

Another underlying theme of this book is, however, that at least some of the principles of education in emergencies could be salutary for easing mainstream education into a more humanitarian position by maximizing the interaction and mutual benefit of formal, non-formal and informal education. Few, if any, have done more for education in emergencies than Margaret Sinclair, and so I have taken her 'Implications for a Humanitarian Response to Education in Emergencies' and the core principles she enunciated in 2001 and reproduced them as Table 4.8. Some of these principles are clearly only directly applicable to an emergency situation but others have a wider significance and potential for application to the mainstream.

| | Conflict and post-conflict | Natural disasters and environmental change | Psychological, medical and health-related issues | Endemic poverty |
|---|---|---|---|---|
| **Included** | Rapid inclusion for some refugees (e.g. Palestinians in Syria and Jordan, most refugees in UK) | Rapid reconnection with mainstream in MDCs (e.g. 2007 floods in England, 2005 floods in Louisiana) | Some HIV/AIDs sufferers in LDCs, most in MDCs. Special needs students in MDCs. Elderly in UK (e.g. U3A) | Some OVCs (e.g. in care homes in UK and Internats in Ukraine). Majority urban poor in MDCs |
| **Marginalized** | Some refugees (e.g. Palestinians in Egypt and IDPs (e.g. in Colombia) | Emergency provision pending reconstruction (e.g. Indian Ocean tsunami and Haiti earthquake victims) | Some HIV/AIDS sufferers in LDCs. Primary carers in MDCs. Victims of industrial disasters (e.g. Bhopal-India and Chernobyl-Ukraine) | Majority rural poor in LDCs. Travellers. Economic migrants in MDCs and LDCs Most OVCs neglected minorities (e.g. Garifuna in Nicaragua) |
| **Excluded** | Refugees in camps (e.g. Karen in Thailand and Palestinians in Lebanon) Persecuted minorities (e.g. Karen in Burma) | Perennial flood victims (e.g. remote delta communities in Bangladesh) | Some HIV/AIDS sufferers in LDCs. Other pandemic sufferers (e.g. malaria and TB) in LDCs | |

*Table 4.7  Inclusion, marginalization, exclusion and situations in relation to the mainstream in more developed (MDCs) and less developed (LDCs) countries*

---

**Core principles for an international consensus**

---

- The right of access of all children and adolescents to education, including post-primary education

- The community-based approach to education represents an investment in future capacity and sustainability in civil society

- Meeting the psychosocial needs of children and adolescents through a range of structured activities

- Rapid responses to meet psychosocial and protection needs

- Relating response to the school year is important in meeting the concerns of affected communities and showing the importance of emergency education to policy-makers and donors

- The principle of education for durable solutions, primarily refugee education in the languages of study used in the area of origin, should be internationally accepted. A regional approach embracing countries of origin and asylum can help to solve problems of textbooks and certification and promote a durable solution – a foundation for positive change

- Including survival and peace-building skills can help save lives and prepare for reconciliation, good government and sustainable development

- The concept of emergency education should be broadened to embrace all the above principles including for all children both in and out of school

- Ensure the participation of special groups: girls, adolescents, those with learning difficulties and physical disabilities, through collaboration with other agencies and community committees

- Ongoing refugee education programmes should be able to respond to, and meet the needs of new refugees

- Make efforts to provide schooling in insecure and remote places

- In prolonged emergencies education quality should improve

- Vigorous field-level partnerships and co-ordination mechanisms are needed to achieve the above objectives

---

*Table 4.8 Margaret Sinclair's implications for a humanitarian response to education in emergencies*

Source: Summarized from Sinclair, 2001

One should first consider all the principles in Table 4.8 in relation to the emergency situations that arise from the range of conflicts and other disasters discussed in this chapter, but those recommended for wider application are:

1    *The right of all children and adolescents to education, including post-primary education.* In the context of mainstream systems of education in more developed countries there are a number of situations in which this right is not recognized. A proportion of refugees and most asylum seekers do not in practice gain access to schooling for their children, or further education for themselves and adult family members. WUS (UK) has made a particular effort to advocate total family access on behalf of the university refugees it supports in Britain. Trafficked people, mostly young women, are often regarded merely as illegal immigrants and, even when in the care of the state through various agencies, fail to receive the educational support they need. The same may apply to unaccompanied minors who may or may not be trafficked.

2    *The community-based approach to education represents an investment in future capacity and sustainability in civil society.* Sometimes the significance of a community-based approach in more developed countries is abandoned in favour of a market-oriented school-choice model, as a result of which the connection of a school with the locality in which it is situated is dislocated. The negative consequences of this for engendering understanding of sustainable development and environmental conservation are discussed in the final chapter.

3    The concept of emergency education should be broadened. This goes back to the point made earlier that 'if we get it right for those with special needs then we likely get it right for all'. Virtually everyone has special needs in terms of education whether of school age or above. Identifying and accommodating these needs should be part of a flexible approach to education, including the point at which a pupil should be reckoned to have reached a certain level of numeracy and literacy. Standardized attainment tests, sometimes accompanied by national targets, are counterproductive to learning. Individual pupil profiling with appropriate support recognizes the individuality of learning and is therefore more likely to foster whatever talents each pupil has, and which may be dormant.

Making sure that education is available to all, that it is community-based to ensure that its potential to encourage and support sustainable development is realized, and taking account of the need to broaden the concept of education are just three areas where mainstream systems are often deficient. So the discussion moves on now to consider other features of dislocation, dysfunctionality and disparity in such systems to which a humanitarian approach needs to be applied as much as to the poor of the marginalized rural majority and those who have experienced disasters of various kinds.

# 5 The Dislocated and Dysfunctional Mainstream

## Chapter outline

## Introduction

As indicated at the outset, the view of education as a humanitarian response espoused in this book is a holistic one. This applies not only to the imperative for all three forms of education to come together, but also in the sense that it is relevant to the mainstream just as much as to those who are excluded or marginalized from it, whether that be routinely, by default or due to disasters. The mainstream is here taken to mean the formal education systems of countries, which normally comprise compulsory and post-compulsory sectors. The compulsory sector, that is to say primary and secondary schooling, is that which governments seek to control most strongly through (1) the legal requirement to attend school up to the earliest leaving age; (2) through access to schools; (3) through the curriculum made available; and (4) through the qualifications that can be gained. Most governments also exert a considerable degree of control on the post-compulsory sector as well. The traditional freedom of universities is in practice often constrained by direct political pressure and/or by funding mechanisms such as those already mentioned relating to research in the UK.

One of the main concerns about education systems, on a global scale, is that they are reckoned to be the desired state of affairs to which those that are excluded or marginalized should be connected, and to which those who have been disrupted by disasters should be reconnected. This is concerning because most mainstream systems exhibit considerable disparity, dislocation and dysfunctionality. Except in situations of political and social revolution, fundamental reform is rare. Even then the four main functions of such systems remain intact: as control mechanisms; to provide knowledge and skills primarily for presumed national economic benefit; to select people for different roles in society; and to provide safe custody while parents are at work. In this chapter these functions will be discussed with regard to issues of (1) structure and funding; (2) access and selection; and (3) curriculum and qualifications.

## Structure and funding of education systems

In almost all countries of the world, attendance of children at school from a given starting age to a minimum leaving age is required by law. This is one of the major aspects of life where the law states what you must do rather than what you must not. Yet many countries, as shown by the EFA Global Monitoring Reports, are still unable to provide a complete system, even at primary level. That is the main reason why there is a marginalized majority of the world's population as far as regular access to schooling is concerned. Enrolment figures are much less an indication of the reality than are attendance figures. There is even more of a disparity when gender is taken into consideration.

Making something a legal requirement that must be partaken of should by rights mean that it is equally available, since all are supposed to be equal under the law. In reality, apart from the fact that in many countries schooling is not yet available to all anyway, even when it is, the structure and funding of the system may give rise to very significant disparities. For example, in the USA, public (i.e. maintained) schooling is the default responsibility of the individual States of the Union and their component school districts, since the constitution of the nation does not include it as a federal responsibility. Public schooling is funded by state taxes and district taxes to about 90 per cent of the total. The remainder comes from federal projects for which states, districts and in some cases individual schools can bid. Overall, the sources of funding for public schooling are approximately: state 40 per cent, district 40 per cent and federal/other 10 per cent. The state and district funding come from taxes that are determined by the voting of the adult population. Inevitably, the tax base varies enormously from place to place within and between the States of the Union. This affects both physical facilities and the salaries of teachers and other educators. For example, the salary of a regular teacher in the affluent district of Enfield, Connecticut, could well exceed that of the superintendent (chief education officer) of the adjacent, relatively poor district of Chicopee, Massachusetts. With there being thousands of school districts in the USA, the disparities of public schooling provision are innumerable and significant, often relating to ethnicity as well. In England, there is not such a degree of local control because, as a result of the 1988 Education Act, the majority of funding has flowed to the individual maintained schools with very little retained by the local authority. Since the turn of the millennium, some state secondary schools have been allowed to apply for 'academy' status, which means that the local authority retains no money at all with respect to them. This inevitably enhances disparity. Furthermore, since the general election of May 2010, a further national policy adjustment in England encourages all primary as well as secondary schools to apply for academy status. This, together with the encouragement to parents to create so-called 'free schools' (i.e. totally free of local authorities), potentially enhances disparity even more, as has been found in Sweden, where this model was pioneered. Whether such disparities within the USA and England are desirable is one matter, but the fact that in the former it arises from decentralized local democratic control over funding and in the latter from centralized national-level control over funding is another. Whatever that means in democratic terms, the outcome is still one of considerable and increasing disparity.

Among the countries of the world there are many different politico-administrative structures and funding mechanisms. At the macro level is the contrast between unitary and federal systems. The USA and UK are examples where the federal level has no direct authority over the component states in the former, and over constituent countries in the latter, especially as far as schooling is concerned. In some other federal structures there are arrangements where primary education is locally/municipally funded, secondary schooling is provincially funded and the tertiary sector is federally funded, with the adult population paying taxes at all levels. This means that the burden of funding schooling, especially at primary level with its much larger clientele, falls disproportionately on local communities, many of which may well be relatively poor, leading to widespread disparity. This creates widely disparate starting lines on the road to upward socio-economic mobility with the aid of schooling. Even in relatively wealthy highly developed nations, most people in the poorest localities don't even get off the starting blocks. This is one of the reasons why comparing the education systems of countries at the national level is nearly always pointless. Many researchers like to concentrate on policy analysis because it is much easier than getting deep into the local milieux and finding out what actually happens on the ground.

At a rather crude level, national systems are often described as centralized or decentralized, but the reasons for, and nature of, the difference may vary. At one end of the scale, in the Chile of Pinochet from 1973 to 1990, a decentralized administration was operated so that the military government could keep maximum control by installing its apparatchiks at local level to ensure conformity as opposed to individual and community initiative. At the other end of the scale are examples of total local community funding of schooling due to the incapacity of the national government to do so. This is the case in many areas of rural sub-Saharan Africa where the combination of lack of government funds, even taking account of international aid, and endemic corruption, leaves many local communities without external financial support for schooling. Mention has already been made of the contribution of some tribal chiefs in Sierra Leone, and other forms of local support, for primary schooling. The situation is extremely disparate. At the same time as local leaders and communities are making valiant efforts to provide and sustain primary schooling, there are also funds being allocated from central governments to 'ghost' schools that no longer exist, or never have. In such contexts a simple school-mapping exercise can reveal anomalies. Even with accurate information, the routine operation of the system is made extremely disparate and often dysfunctional by the very poor quality of the infrastructure. Inspection of schools and distribution of books and other materials may be extremely irregular, leading to major disparities in the routine operation of the system. This applies not only to swathes of rural Africa, South Asia and Latin America, but also to developing tropical island archipelago nations. In some such examples in the South Pacific the massive swell of the ocean can cause an imposed remoteness even though the distances involved may not be great. The state of the ocean is not the only factor in such locations, as Evelyn Joseph reports with respect to the Republic of the Marshall Islands (RMI) (2009):

> The geography of many island nations – schools spread across numerous and remote islands – presents one the biggest stumbling blocks to school improvement. The isolation of schools has a major impact on the RMI Ministry of Education's (MOE's) to adequately support and monitor many schools. Transportation represents the biggest challenge. Of the 82 public schools – 76 primary and 6 secondary – only 17 have consistent access to supplies and

services from the MOE. In the last year, numerous challenges faced by both air and sea transportation services, including rising fuel costs, have made the situation even more acute.

(Joseph, 2009, 9–10)

The role of organized religion in the evolution and operation of systems of education has also been mentioned above. As far as issues of structure and funding are concerned, such bodies are still extremely influential in many countries, developed and underdeveloped. Returning to the USA, from the founding of the nation, religion was explicitly separated from public schooling at both primary and secondary levels. Nonetheless, religious bodies, predominantly Catholic, have been permitted to operate schools outside the public system. These have been termed 'parochial schools' and in effect form a system of their own, under diocesan control. Because of their religious identity they receive no public funds, and so depend on relatively low-level fees from parents. In England, the opposite occurred with religious, especially Anglican and later Catholic, authorities being the formative agents behind a national system of schooling. They are still important components of that system, with between a quarter and a third of the maintained schools in England overall. Both denominations operate diocesan control, being responsible for the upkeep of their buildings and land but with the majority cost, teacher's salaries, paid by the state. With local authorities still, at the time of writing, having some influence, and both Anglican and Catholic dioceses involved, this is a complicated picture, necessarily involving disparities.

At the tertiary level, there is another contrast between the USA and the UK with respect to the contribution of religious bodies to the foundation and operation of colleges and universities. Although in the UK such bodies were very significant in the foundation of the so-called renaissance universities, their influence was challenged by the foundation of the first secular college, University College London, by the utilitarian movement in 1826. Although the Anglican Church responded rapidly by establishing King's College London in 1829 and University College, Durham in 1832, the subsequent founding of universities of a technical and instrumental nature in a succession of rapidly growing industrial cities resulted in the emergence of a secular network in which no private university existed until the foundation of the University of Buckingham in 1983, which still remains the only such institution. By contrast, in the USA, the many universities related to religious organizations are necessarily private. In addition to the many Catholic foundations there are concentrations related to other denominations such as Lutheran in Minnesota and Baptist in North Carolina.

In the main zones of the developing world there is again contrast between the numerous Catholic universities in Latin America and the more varied religious-related establishments in sub-Saharan Africa and South Asia. But in some cases the input and influence of religious bodies may be considerable. For example, in Uganda almost all schools in the national system are provided by the major Christian denominations, with their own diocesan considerations. In the Far East, originally Christian-mission-founded colleges such as Peking University in Beijing have mostly become secular. In East Central Asia where the earliest universities in the world were founded, long before the emergence of the major Abrahamic religions, as well as in the Middle East, Islam strongly influences the structure of higher education, especially in Iran, which is virtually a theocracy. By contrast, the top Western institutions in the region were and are secular foundations like the American University of Beirut (1866) and the American University of Cairo (1919).

Intertwined with issues of state and religious foundation and funding of school systems and higher education institutions is that of disparities created by the public/private dichotomy. In the worlds of developed Western nations, especially in Europe, private institutions, usually religious related, predated state school systems. In the USA, the private school sector forms a third branch parallel to the public and parochial systems, with each being separate from the other two. There are also many private universities and colleges, including the elite 'Ivy League' institutions such as Harvard, Yale, Columbia and Princeton. In the UK, as mentioned above, there is only one private university, Buckingham, a relatively recent foundation which it was hoped by the neo-liberal Conservative government of the day would be the forerunner of many. However, in contrast to the USA, the secondary school sector in the UK, and especially England, has a very strong private component. Containing about 8 per cent of the school-age population, this sector succeeds in gaining a disproportionate number of places at the most prestigious universities, supplying about 50 per cent of the undergraduates at Oxford and Cambridge alone. These two universities provide an interesting anomaly in that while they are state universities, their colleges are independent private institutions, the oldest enjoying considerable accumulated wealth.

The independent schools sector in the UK, most of which is in England, operates according to a different temporal structure from that of the maintained sector, and does not have to follow the national curriculum or take the same public examinations. Most maintained school systems make their main primary/secondary break at eleven while the private sector does so at fourteen. Most students remain in one sector or the other, so that two completely separate paths are followed from an early age. This has social as well as political implications. Lasting friendships are made during schooldays and are maintained though adulthood as well, a major factor in maintaining the strong social class dimension of English society. Freedom for independent schools to take whatever examinations they like means that many choose the prestigious International General Certificate of Education and/or the International Baccalaureate. Universities, especially the prestigious elite group, recognize and favour the quality of these programmes and awards, which disadvantages the majority-maintained school applicants who have mostly not had the opportunity to follow them. Whether early indications at the time of writing that the newly elected (May 2010) UK coalition government will open up freedom of choice of curricula and examinations for maintained schools in England will be fulfilled remains to be seen. If so, it will remove a structural disparity but may produce a different scale of disparity as individual maintained schools make their choices.

Not all countries have the same degree or type of public/private disparity in schooling as the UK, but all countries in the world have their elites who know how to work education systems to their own advantage. For example, in the 1960s the USA supported what it called the Alliance for Progress with some of the countries of South America. One of the components of this initiative was education, with financial support for boosting the state sector of schooling and providing more opportunities for upward social mobility and qualifications acquisition. At the time, in that region, girls were even more disadvantaged than today and it was hoped that the Alliance for Progress would help to produce an opportunity to address the gender imbalance in the professions. To some extent it did, but the elites saw the opportunity to educate their daughters at public expense rather than, as previously, on the private 'finishing school' circuit. As it happens, this appropriation did have some benefits as a generation of elite women later emerged on the professional and political scene with, in general, rather more liberal views and actions than their more reactionary forbears.

Globally, as well as at the national level, concern is growing rapidly over the massive increase in recent decades of private universities, especially in developing countries. One of the most striking legacies of the neo-liberal economic trends of the past three decades or so has been the proliferation of private universities, especially in developing countries. As already indicated, there is nothing problematic about private universities or schools per se. In free societies they have to be allowed to exist and will only do so, and survive, if there is a market for them. Concern arises when either schools or universities in the private sector create significant imbalance in their sector. This is the case much more in the tertiary sector. In Latin America, especially, there has been a massive growth of mostly substandard private universities and colleges. Some high-standard private universities already existed in the region, but the majority of the new foundations range from the sub-standard to the criminally fraudulent. Brazil, being the most populous and rapidly developing country in the region, has seen this development to a greater extent than most, and has struggled to regulate it. As Maria Castro (2004) points out:

> Brazilian higher education shares some of the general characteristics highlighted in the international literature, reviewed above; it receives very little or no public resources; most institutions are non-university teaching places, clustered at the lower end of the academic quality continuum; they face harsh competition; and receive the least educated students. Typically these are older than average, are the first generation of their families to get to higher education, and attend evening courses because they are already in the workforce.
>
> (Castro, 2004, 185)

She goes on to mention a number of initiatives and regulations introduced by the Brazilian government to police the private higher education institutions, including controlling the award of university status, periodic renewal of accreditation if standards are maintained, capping tuition fees, laws regarding philanthropy, and the veracity of promotional literature. So Brazil is dealing seriously with the growth of private higher education because the government understands that it is necessary for the realization of the capacity the country needs for high-level labour to be developed. Some of the other, smaller and poorer, Latin American countries have found this difficult to contain, or do not have the political will to do so. The Dominican Republic is a case in point. Here the number of private 'universities' is out of all proportion to the scale of the country. Its location in the Caribbean region leads on to consideration of the number of so-called offshore private universities and colleges spawned by the USA private sector in the Anglophone Caribbean. This has been going on for at least thirty years, following the establishment of St George's University School of Medicine in Grenada in 1977, the security of which was used as a pretext for the bombing of the island by the USA in 1983, due to concern about Cuba assisting Grenada with adult literacy programmes and the building of an airport to boost tourism. The very mixed picture of tertiary education in the region is presented in Lopze-Segrera et al. (2009).

The proliferation of private universities and colleges extends way beyond the New World to Africa and especially Asia, and has been of particular concern to UNESCO since at least 1998. Unlike primary and secondary schools, the tertiary sector is difficult for governments of poorer countries to control. China (PRC), with its dual political economy of neo-liberal capitalism and strong political control by the Communist Party, manages to regulate the spate of private universities, while putting its support behind making sure that the top state universities, such as Peking, Fudan and Tsinghua, climb up the international table of the top hundred universities in the world. Smaller and weaker developing countries are unable or unwilling to contain this least appetizing product of the market era of international economics, and so a succession of UNESCO global forums of higher education has kept it on the agenda, including on that of the 2009 World Conference on Higher Education in Paris. The report of that meeting, under the title *Trends in Global Higher Education: Tracking an Academic Revolution* (2009), catalogues and explains the remarkable growth of private higher education worldwide over the past four decades or so. While acknowledging the earlier developments of this phenomenon in Latin America and especially Brazil, the authors point out that Asia, and especially East Asia, has the largest private higher education sector of all major regions, with several countries noting over 70 per cent of tertiary sector enrolments in private institutions: Indonesia, Japan, the Philippines and South Korea. Malaysia is at about 50 per cent, as are Iran and Kazakhstan, with India just above 30 per cent and Pakistan just below it. Post-communist Eastern Europe has shown considerable increases in private higher education since 1990, while sub-Saharan Africa, Nigeria, Uganda and Kenya have significant private sectors at this level.

The 2009 UNESCO report explains that privatization includes not only strictly private universities and colleges, but also the increasing trend in almost all countries, including the most developed, for the public sector to be augmenting its income from private sources of various kinds: alumni contributions, sponsors in the industrial and commercial field, research grants from companies and charitable trusts, and fees from higher degree students, increasingly from other countries. This is partly because, as countries develop and move towards some degree of mass higher education, they cannot afford to fund the expansion from public funds alone. Some of the pressure comes from sheer increased demand from secondary-school graduates who realize that in the increasingly knowledge-based economies of their countries, gaining employment will depend on having achieved at least a bachelor's-level degree. Pressure also comes from the somewhat invidious international higher education league tables, which, as with TIMMS and PISA at lower secondary level, tend to fixate governments to an unfortunate degree. Such rankings are even more methodologically dubious than their secondary-level counterparts, with major institutions such as the Sorbonne, Berlin and Salamanca absent due to their not operating primarily in English. Whether it is wise for universities such as Peking, Tsinghua and Fudan in China to expend such efforts to climb the anglophone tree is a moot point. Be that as it may, the outcome of both international and intranational rankings of universities exhibit major disparities.

Within the developing world most private schools have a religious identity as well and in general are less prestigious and separate from their public-sector counterparts than those in wealthy Western countries. In India, however, there has been a long-established tradition of private schooling, partly derived from the benefaction of traditional rulers, partly due to religiously based philanthropy, and partly due to the legacy of the British Raj. In the last few decades, the private sector in India has seen a remarkable engagement with the public sector in assisting with the engagement of the rural poor in primary and secondary schooling. This is also related to the marketization of education encouraged by the Indian government, as is the parallel growth of private education in the PRC, which has no such historic, aristocratic or colonial roots.

Sometimes the private dimension is seen in the form of corporate involvement, a movement which was very influential during the growth of the economic power of the USA after the civil war and into the twentieth century. Even today, regional business and education alliances exist to try to enhance the quality of school leavers entering the employment market. In some countries, notably Japan, massive corporations have dominated schools and universities in locations where they have major operations. They instil a company work ethic in their schools and universities that translates smoothly into their workforce generation by generation.

Because of the highly academic origins and traditions of the European model of formal education, which has become the global norm, resulting system structures involve notions of status. Almost everywhere this has favoured the academic area of learning as opposed to the technical. This has resulted in the technical and vocational dimensions of learning becoming the poor relations within many systems. There are exceptions, most notably in Germany, where the Realschule option reflected the success of the technical dimension of its economic history, and in Russia, where the legacy of the former Soviet ten-year polytechnical school remains. In most other developed countries, the technical and vocational dimension is mainly represented as a post-compulsory option open to all above the school-leaving age. In the USA, this takes the form of the community college sector, while in England it is the further education sector. Both form an alternative route to university, as well as providing sub-degree technical and vocational programmes leading to the acquisition of a range of skills from plumbing to English as a second language. In both countries, these are mostly public-sector colleges, but in England they are no longer under local authority control but instead under that of a national funding council. This means they are part of a loose nationwide network and no longer structurally related to their geographical locality, making for greater potential disparity.

Because of the colonial legacy of the European model, this technical and vocational model carried its low status with it into all regions of the developing world. Given the dearth of funding and degree of underdevelopment in this world of the marginalized majority, it is rarely represented as a sector. Along with the equally disparate nature of adult education, and incomplete secondary sectors, this leaves a massive gap that can only be partially filled by the immigration of skilled and trained labour and/or non-formal agencies. As illustrated above, excellent interventions are being made by NGOs: for example, Practical Action in the area of intermediate technology and ActionAid in meaningful literacy acquisition. But NGOs cannot be expected to build and sustain a sector of provision across whole nations, especially as they rely for their funding on irregular and insecure donations from the governments, agencies and individuals of the developed countries in which they are based. In those countries, a massive non-formal education and training contribution is routinely made, though rarely appreciated as such, by employers in both private and public sectors. Although not entirely absent in the developing world, the extractive, manufacturing and service sectors of national economies are much less developed, and scattered in locational terms. So although, for example, some mining companies in Southern Africa and oil companies in equatorial Africa do provide skills training, it rarely extends outside their own workforce to local communities, though they sometimes provide schooling for the children of their employees.

After the agricultural revolution and the industrial revolution we are now well into the cybernetic revolution, one of the main features of which is the emergence of the 'knowledge business'. The networks of most academics are now at least cross-national and often global in proportion, even in the most arcane disciplines. One of the more basic features of the knowledge business is the establishment of offshoots of a parent university in other countries. The aforementioned St George's Medical School in Grenada is a case in point; it has now become a multi-discipline campus. Several American universities have campuses in the UK, while several UK universities have campuses in the upper end of the developing

countries' market, such as Nottingham University's Ningbo
China and another in Malaysia. Many other UK universities
from developed countries run programmes overseas without
permanent base in the countries concerned. Hull's aforemention
programme of teacher education in the British Virgin Islands is a case in
point. Sometimes a number of universities concentrate their efforts at the
same location such as in the 'university city' in Dohar, Qatar in the Gulf,
where several American universities are operating a small range of degree
programmes. This is reckoned to be good business for Qatar, which is
aiming to be a regional hub for higher education.

In addition to such 'offshore' initiatives, many universities are offering
full or partial on-line degree programmes on a global scale. Their standards
range from very high to very low, and clients need to take great care in
checking the credibility of a programme before embarking on it. These
cross-border programmes along with overseas campuses are obvious
examples of trading in knowledge and have attracted the attention of
the General Agreement on Trade and Services (GATS), which came
into being in 1995 under the auspices of the World Trade Organization
(WTO). Education was excluded from the GATS if it operated under
non-market conditions. So, for example, the flow of overseas students to
UK's public universities, vital to their financial well-being, would not be
seen as a market, though in fact it is. However, with the flow of cross-
border services on the scale that has subsequently occurred, the trade in
knowledge has become an issue of critical debate. For example, Abbott
(2009) points out that:

> It has been argued that trade in education services ensures access to
> high quality education for both international and domestic students
> because the GATS foreign education providers are flourishing and
> these providers will meet the skills and training outcomes. The
> intensifying trade in education services, however, has served to
> highlight the groups who have access to education and those who
> do not. Education increasingly becomes a competitive commodity
> and as such the question arises of 'will education become less
> accessible to all?'
>
> (Abbott, 2009, 7)

After a thorough review of the literature in relation to this type of concern,
she concludes that: 'Even though the GATS focuses on higher education
and the EFA does not focus on higher education, privatisation, user pays
and the reduction of public expenditure in education hinder the equal
access to education' (15). This is not likely to be true of the compulsory

stage of the formal education systems of developed countries, but it could be an issue for their less developed counterparts with incomplete systems in the world of the marginalized majority. It could increase the disparity in such countries between the elite and the mass of the population already evident in the digital divide. In some developing countries, notably India, there are significant innovations in privately provided primary schooling in poor rural areas, as well as private/public partnerships. But even there, the rate of population increase makes it unlikely that there will be any convergence between movement towards EFA and the availability of private services in the post-secondary centre. More likely there may be clusters of population where this convergence could occur, leading to even more marked spatial disparities in education than exist already.

In the context of education as a humanitarian response, incompleteness and disparity of provision in any sector severely compromise the ideal of a holistic, integrated and appropriate education. This is further exacerbated by issues of access and selection.

# Access and selection

Issues of access and selection are intricately interconnected and contribute to disparity and dysfunctionality in the mainstream systems of education in both developed and developing countries. In a complete system where enrolment and attendance at school, at least up to the end of the compulsory sector, are a legal requirement, it has to be assumed that primary and secondary schools are made available to all. This is normally the case but there is considerable disparity in terms of their accessibility in geographical terms, and selection is one of the main factors involved.

As mentioned above, selection is one of the prime functions of formal education systems. Earl Hopper in his seminal paper on 'A Typology for the Classification of Education Systems' (1968), built on Ralph Turner's notions of 'contest and sponsored mobility', which were conceived in terms only of a comparison between the education systems of the USA and UK. He agrees with Turner that these two modes of selection, the former by open competition and the latter by invitation, are based on the folk norms of the respective societies. Whereas the English state system was developed from the model of the pre-existing private schools of the elite, that of the USA was based on a meritocratic model of social mobility for a new society. Hopper proceeded to develop this theme to a point where it could be applied to most if not all developed national systems by adding additional criteria to Turner's aristocratic and meritocratic: namely, communistic and paternalistic. This quartet related to the question, ' Who should be selected?' This he reckoned to be based on either universalistic or particularistic criteria. Then he asked the question, 'Why should they be selected?' This he reckoned to be based on collectivistic or individualistic criteria. Although somewhat convoluted and jargon-ridden, Hopper's contribution was important because he rightly recognized the fundamentally cultural basis of education in any society and the issue of selection within it. Figure 5.1 is based on Hopper's diagrammatic representation of his typology.

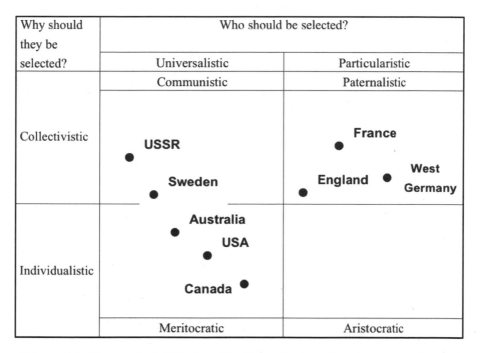

*Figure 5.1 Hopper's 1968 classification of educational systems based on their criteria for selection*

Source: Adapted from Hopper, 1968

Although based on the systems of developed countries, because of the global export of the European model through colonization and colonialism, the same criteria for selection could be applied to many of the systems of developing countries. Almost all societies have their elites, mostly urban-based, who control the system of education and those selected to advance through it.

At the macro level there is a dichotomy between urban and rural areas. In less developed countries this tends to be more clear-cut, whereas in the more urbanized industrialized nations there are larger intermediate situations such as suburbs and exurbs. For obvious reasons, schools are more accessible in urban areas, not only because a high population density requires more primary and secondary schools, but also because modes of transportation, private and public, are more readily available. There are also likely to be more private schools available in the urban areas of all countries, as the owners of such schools depend on a threshold market population with sufficient disposable income. This is generally the case, but where, as in England, there is a tradition of boarding in the more prestigious private schools, an urban location is not necessarily an issue. This prestigious private sector of schooling in England is unusually large and influential, comprising two stages: preparatory or 'prep' schools, up to the age of fourteen, followed by secondary schools which, if the headteacher is deemed acceptable to the 'Headmaster's Conference', are termed 'public' schools. This is confusing and anachronistic even by the standards of eccentricity inherent in the convoluted growth of schooling in England. However, the issue is pertinent here because access to the preparatory and secondary schools of the private sector occurs at different ages from the state, or maintained, school sector. This is significant because whereas the general population does not have access to the private sector because of relative absence of wealth, connections and family tradition, the opposite is not the case because the wealthy, having paid their taxes, have the right to access or re-access the state school system at any time. With the onset of an economic recession since 2007, a significant number of parents are taking this option, a point that has relevance for the issue of school choice.

School choice, a component of neo-liberal economics in the form of marketization, is a very contested policy when it comes to access to schooling during the compulsory education phase in any country in which it operates. National networks of primary and secondary schooling were originally developed to serve existing communities. Each school had a delineated catchment area, smaller for primary schools, which were normally non-selective, also giving consideration to the limited mobility of young children and their parents, often with other siblings in tow. For secondary schools the catchments were larger due to the increased mobility of their pupils. That was the simple model based on communities. However, where forms of selection for secondary education existed, such as the Eleven Plus examination for entry to grammar schools in England, the connection with communities was only retained in small towns with a single co-educational grammar school, or one each for boys and for girls. In larger towns and cities where a larger number of grammar schools existed, sometimes quite proximate for historic reasons of their foundation, there were overlapping catchments, again further complicated by the incidence of co-educational and single sex schools. Selection was then made on the basis of (1) performance in the Eleven Plus examination; (2) parental preference; and (3) the number of places available in each grammar school in the area. For those who were not selected, that is to say the vast majority, places were available in secondary modern schools on a neighbourhood, i.e. community, catchment basis. In Hopper's terms that system, at its peak between about 1950 and 1975, would be paternalistic because of its derivation, and collectivistic because it was ostensibly a national selection system. In practice, it concealed two massive injustices and innumerable disparities. The first injustice was to girls who, because of their overall superior performance at that age had to have their grades reduced to a point where a 50:50 situation of 'passes' was achieved. This was passed off as being some kind of equality in this *rite de passage* towards the professions. The second injustice was more class-oriented in that the test itself was of the verbal reasoning kind. This favoured children with what Basil Bernstein called an elaborated code of facility in English, that is to say the vocabulary and usage of the middle classes. The innumerable disparities that occurred were due to anomalies of political geography in the relationship between local authority boundaries, demographic realities, and the locational legacy of grammar school foundations. An example of this is shown in Figure 5.2, which represents the situation in the area between Kingston-upon-Hull and the East Riding of Yorkshire around 1970.

In most parts of England, selective secondary schooling was phased out between 1965 and 1975, and replaced by various models of non-selective secondary schooling, or 'comprehensive schools', as they were popularly known. The objective was to have secondary schools relate to their immediate locality, be it urban, rural or a mix of the two. But with a change of government in 1979 favouring selection again, the neo-liberal marketization model was invoked through the mechanism of parental choice. This meant that parents could opt for their local secondary school by a certain deadline, or opt for another secondary school in their local authority area, or opt for such a school in another local authority area. This was of course a flawed market model, because unlike a normal market in goods, schools could not expand and contract at will. Their maximum numbers were set by health and safety regulations, and for a market to operate there would have to be excess capacity. Figures 5.3a and 5.3b illustrate the situation at the Hull/East Yorkshire interface in 1980 and 2000.

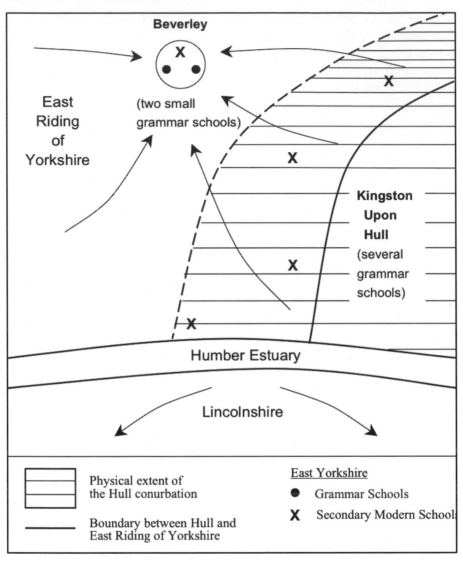

*Figure 5.2 Secondary school selection at the East Yorkshire/Kingston-upon-Hull interface circa 1970*

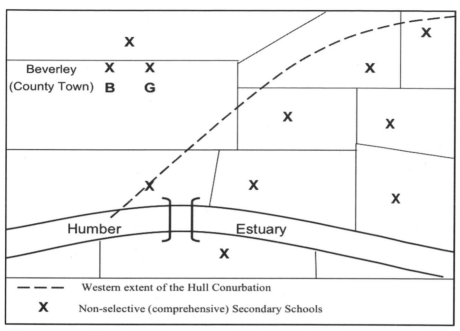

Figure 5.3a *National catchment areas of secondary schools in the unified County of Humberside 1988*

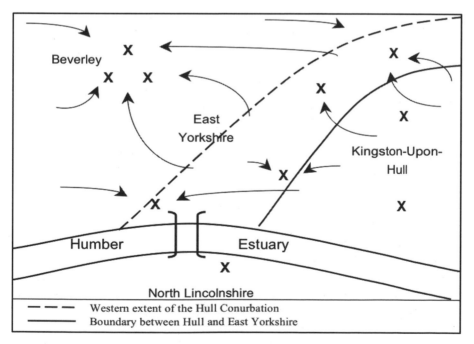

Figure 5.3b *Post-2000 situation of school choice in the area after further local authority reorganization*

Although the modes of selection and their implications for disparity in the English context illustrated in Figures 5.2 and 5.3 do not have exact parallels elsewhere, some form of selection for secondary schooling exists in broadly comparable countries. In the USA, where the notion of the marketization of public schooling originated, each of the fifty States of the Union made its own decision as to whether or not to go down that path. Some decided to remain with the long-standing common, or community school model of Horace Mann dating from the early nineteenth century, that is to say the non-selective high school. However, as indicated in the previous section on structure and funding, in the USA in most urban and suburban areas there are parochial and private high schools as well. So although no structural system of selection exists in this situation, access decisions can be made by the parents, and also the individual parochial or private schools to which they apply. Some of the states of the USA did decide on the marketization model of school choice, most notably Massachusetts, whose Education Reform Act of 1993 was closely modelled on parts of the 1988 Education Reform Act of England and Wales. The Massachusetts legislation required each school district to operate school choice for access to high schools, and also made it an option for any school district to agree cross-border school choice with its neighbours. As already indicated, for school choice to be possible in practice there has to be a situation of spare capacity in at least some schools. This can be achieved by (1) a demographic shortfall leaving some schools with spare places; (2) the creation of new schools; and (3) the extension of the buildings of existing schools. The most common way of creating capacity in those states of the USA favouring school choice was to allow the creation of a new type of public school known as a charter school. States in favour of this option would announce a maximum number of charters for which interested groups of adults could apply. Groups that formed to make such applications would have a common interest to promote a school with a special feature such as an emphasis on science or on the creative and performing arts. They would have to follow the normal state curriculum, but organize their time in such a way as to allow for their particular emphasis to be accommodated. The state, having awarded the charter for a limited period of time, typically three years, would fund the teachers but would not provide a building. The interest group would sometimes take over the buildings of a school that had been closed, or hire a local or church hall. Charter schools can be primary or secondary in some states. The next issue is to decide on a fair means of selection in which enrolment is not controlled by the group holding the charter. Many such schools hold lotteries and hold strictly to the outcome. The writer witnessed such a lottery in North Carolina where, as it happened, the children of two of the members of the interest group failed to be selected. They had to accept it and send their offspring elsewhere. Local democracy lies at the heart of American public school provision and access. Charter schools, like all others in a school district, come under the jurisdiction of the superintendent (chief education officer) who is appointed by the mayor and other elected members. The superintendent and local government can therefore encourage charter schools as a way of creating the additional capacity without which school choice cannot work. In some areas it has worked, in others it has not. At the time of writing (June 2010) the new coalition government in UK – with education jurisdiction only over England – is proposing to allow interest groups to set up so-called 'free schools' without any relation to local democratic control, as well as encouraging existing maintained schools to become academies, also free of local democratic control. Both in the USA and England, these developments create further disparity, whether answerable to local or to national democratic control.

Access to the mainstream and/or particular schools within it is not only an issue in predominantly urbanized developed countries. In rural areas, even in such countries, and certainly in the world of the marginalized majority, distance is a telling factor. The incomplete and disparate nature of primary school distribution often makes schools difficult to reach without the transportation facilities enjoyed in more developed countries. Children may have to walk miles to school and back, assuming there is one available and they are eligible. It is often the case that girls, and sometimes boys, have the early morning task of collecting water for the family each day. This may also be a matter of miles even before the walk to school is undertaken. It is one of the factors leading to non-enrolment, especially of girls, in such areas, as well as to intermittent attendance and eventually wastage. Access and attendance are not just a function of distance or regulations: parental decision is a key factor. Survival as a family, and to some extent community, matter, and while formal schooling for some may be beneficial in the long run, it is a gamble against the opportunity cost of the loss of any child's contribution. Consequently, access decisions are made by parents, and that usually means fathers. In their research for DfID on factors affecting the participation of girls in primary education, Colin Brock and Nadine Cammish (1997) found that while geographical factors were certainly apparent, the two most influential issues were poverty and patriarchy. While, as has been discussed above, innovative NGOs such as BRAC in Bangladesh, can make a difference where they are working, neither they nor the countries they operate in yet have the capacity to make appropriate primary, secondary and adult education a sustainable reality for all. That is most likely decades away.

It is not just the vast rural areas and populations of tropical Latin America, sub-Saharan Africa and mainland Asia that encounter such problems of access to schooling. There are some very remote parts of developed countries as well, such as northern Canada, the Australian outback and Siberian Russia. But those nations have the capacity to go some way to ensuring access using modern technology.

There are in the world a significant number of island nations, large and small, some of which are archipelago states. We have already discussed the difficulties facing educational provision and inspection in such situations with respect to a small Pacific island nation. In the larger cases, such as the Philippines, Indonesia and even Fiji, the main islands can offer access for most to primary and sometimes secondary schools, depending on the selection situation. But on smaller outer islands it may only be possible to cover primary schooling. Considerations of maturity and safety may well cause parents to refuse to send their children to secondary schools many miles away across the water even if places are available. Such a situation may be further complicated by disparities of language. In the Pacific archipelago nation of Vanuatu, for example, which has scores of islands, over a hundred indigenous languages are spoken in addition to the three official languages of Bislama, English and French. Each indigenous language has a maximum number of 2,000 native speakers. Although this is the most extreme example in the world, linguistic disparities are commonplace in geographically dislocated populations, including among the marginalized majority in continental mainland locations.

Vanuatu is also an example of a small state, a category normally reckoned to be of fewer than 2 million people. Many, like Vanuatu, have populations of 250,000 or fewer. There are advantages and disadvantages arising from small national scale as far as access to formal education is concerned. If the small country is a single-island (Barbados), littoral (the Gambia) or landlocked (Lesotho) state there is less difficulty in providing primary education for all than in larger territories. In the Commonwealth Caribbean islands, this was mostly achieved a century before the Millennium Development Goals were invented, followed by selective secondary schools on the English grammar school model. However, the proportion of schools to total population varied enormously depending on the relative activity of religious bodies in establishing schools. Some islands, such as Barbados and Grenada, acquired relatively more grammar schools and consequently sent more students to university and the professions than others.

Access and selection issues do not apply only to primary and secondary schooling. Because of their small scale, such nations have to use larger ones for their further and higher education requirements. Traditionally, small island nations in what was then the British West Indies would send undergraduates to the UK, USA and Canada. Then in 1948, the University of the West Indies was founded, initially as a University College of the University of London, with campuses in Jamaica, Barbados and Trinidad, and began to take the majority of candidates from the countries that now constitute the Commonwealth Caribbean. This enabled more undergraduates to access a university degree programme and to remain in the region. In 1962, the University of the South Pacific was founded in Suva, Fiji, with a second campus in Western Samoa, and an outreach programme to the smaller island nations of the region. More recently, in both regions, community colleges have been founded in the various nations feeding into these regional universities This enables even more local undergraduates to access degree programmes in their own island before moving on to the main campuses in the final year(s). Some relatively small territories in wealthier locations, such as Singapore, Hong Kong and more recently 'The Gulf', have invested heavily in higher education in order to be the hub of spheres of influence in the new age of the global knowledge industry. This not only attracts students and investment from outside, but also provides expanded access for their local populations to higher education programmes.

With the cybernetic revolution, access to higher education, or even schooling, does not necessarily have to require a physical presence at a school or college. In very remote locations such as the Australian outback and the Falkland Islands, children of school age were long taught by peripatetic teachers travelling by horseback or light aircraft. Now they have their own computers and can access on-line programmes. This can also be done in the more remote locations in developed countries such as the islands of the Outer Hebrides in Scotland, where university outreach programmes emanate from Inverness and Glasgow. Although innovative programmes of teacher education in the rural marginalized majorities of the developing world, such as the TESSA programme described above, are making a significant contribution, in most other areas of further and higher education the majority of young people and adults has yet to access suitable programmes on-line. At the level of inter-university collaboration and third-country development projects, however, the considerable potential of higher education institutions (HEIs) to assist meaningful local development through ICT is beginning to be recognized, as illustrated at the 2009 UNESCO World Conference on Higher Education and especially the report of the Commonwealth of Learning (2009):

> Over a period of time, HEIs along with civil society have questioned the conventional transfer of technology models in the developmental process and have begun to emphasise indigenous knowledge and interactive learning empowerment of the communities. In

many countries programmes like National Social Service (NSS) and youth programmes are raising students' awareness of the social dimensions of development. Unlike University–Industry linkages and technology transfer, which are continuously monitored, the linkages between HEIs and community have yet to be tracked in a systematic manner.

(Commonwealth of Learning, 2009, 13)

Despite the caveat in the final sentence, this is a clear step in the right direction to try to ensure the relevance of any educational and training innovation by testing it through the local culture, and hopefully expanding the cultural capacity so that any development gain can be sustained. The key issue here is the recognition that formal education, in this case through the medium of ICT, can only play its part if it is in harmony with the non-formal and informal, possibly indigenous, educational culture of the society in question. This brings us to the consideration of a third dimension of disparity and dysfunctionality in the mainstream: curriculum and qualifications.

## Curriculum and qualifications

In preparing this book, I have not been averse to bucking contemporary academic fashion and draw on some sources from decades ago, as well as more recent ones. From time to time particularly perceptive publications occur, and for this component of the discussion of disparity and dysfunctionality few sources could be more helpful than Ronald Dore's *The Diploma Disease* (1976) and John Oxenham's edited volume *Education Versus Qualifications* (1984). Both titles encapsulate the problem brilliantly and their contents are still just as relevant, since the problems to which they refer have not gone away. Neither are they likely to do so for some time to come, such is the inertia and control of the educational establishment everywhere, which is why education is a global concern.

Qualifications such as the renaissance 'master of arts' degree were granted at a time when the title meant not only passing an examination, but also the recognition of a person fit to impart wisdom as well as information. With the massive growth of the world's population has come credentialism, a way of qualifying individuals for selection to undertake technical tasks or of acquiring the necessary status to display diffuse skills in the professions. However, as indicated by Hopper's criteria for selection, this is mediated through folk-norms and ideologies such as meritocracy, paternalism and communism.

Ronald Dore's concept of a 'diploma disease' was based largely, though not entirely, on how the issues of assessment of academic success, certification of that success, and selection for different jobs were affecting the purpose and quality of formal education in developing countries. In general, he came to the conclusion that the effect of those issues was adverse, and recommended some suggestions for radical reform. The main focus of Dore's discourse, and this is followed up in Oxenham's book, to which he contributed, is the role of selection and certification in the relationship between formal education and allocation of its products to different forms of employment. He was concerned about the same thing as A.C. Grayling, quoted above, which is the adverse effect on schooling of, above all else, seeking a direct investment-type relationship between it and the national economy. Ronald Dore advocated two radical reforms to counter it: (1) begin careers earlier – after basic schooling – and leave selection to occur within employment rather than before it; recourse to post-school education and training would be 'on the job' involving further and higher education institutions as and when appropriate along the way; and (2) selection procedures should avoid learning-achievement assessments in favour of forms of testing which cannot be crammed for, such as aptitude tests. However desirable such alternatives may be, they still face a range of reactionary forces so ingrained as to be virtually endemic decades after Nigel Brooke and John Oxenham identified them. Their criticisms were as follows: (1) 'education in developing countries is viewed almost exclusively in instrumental, qualification gathering terms'; (3) 'existing techniques of assessing academic success both militate decisively against reforms in curricula and pedagogy, and more important are incapable of substantive improvement'; (4) the anxiety of parents about their children's success 'affects teachers' behaviour conservatively and constitutes an inhibition to reform (Oxenham, 1984, 147–8).

While the concerns rightly expressed by their authors above were presented with reference to what I have here called the world of the marginalized majority, they can equally well be applied to the educational world from which they emanate, that of the disparate and dysfunctional mainstream of developed nations. The words of the Jamaican economist G.L. Beckford (1972), with respect to plantation societies of former colonies of European powers, that 'the most intractable problem of dependent societies is the colonised condition of the minds of the people', could just as well apply to the extent to which a partial and limited view of education, derived from only one of its three forms, has defined the culture of schooling worldwide. A particular mindset has been generated that has profound consequences for curricular priorities that have become conventions.

The concept of 'knowledge being one and indivisible' is popularly related to Plato's theory of knowledge, but he was also referring back to previous discourse on the issue involving Socrates and others some fifty years earlier in the fifth century BC of classical Athens. In the era of modern education, a similar concept was put forward by the philosopher Alfred North Whitehead in 1929 in the subtitle of his book *Whitehead on the Philosophy of Education: The Seamless Coat of Learning*. That is why the standard doctoral degree is, and has long been known as, doctor of philosophy (PhD), irrespective of the field in which the research has been carried out. Epistemology, the theory of knowledge, is not primarily concerned with subjects and disciplines but rather with approaches such as empiricism, constructivism and rationalism, which are to do with knowledge acquisition. With universities having preceded schools in the evolution of educational institutions, the emergence and definition of identified components of knowledge was handed down, as it were, piecemeal according to what was deemed appropriate learning at the time. With the Christian, especially Catholic, Church being a key player in the foundations of the European model of education and in the emergence of the political administration of territory, subjects such as Latin, religion, philosophy, music and mathematics comprised the school curricula of the day. Over the centuries, and especially with the development of the European nation state and its component school system, and with the establishment and institutionalization of new disciplines in the universities, some of these, such as history and geography, began to be added to the school curriculum. Exploration and industrialization in the eighteenth and nineteenth centuries enhanced the claims of the natural sciences, physics, chemistry and biology. Hence the so-called balanced curriculum of the elite secondary schools emerged and was in due course disseminated to the mainstream systems of universal primary and secondary schooling.

There is nothing wrong with the existence of these subjects in the curriculum of formal schooling per se. Rather, what is of concern is the cult of specialization that has characterized them in the universities and in the world of schoolteaching with its related associations of subject teachers maintaining their distance from others. All this has been handed down to the younger countries, many yet to emerge from the legacy of colonialism with hopefully fresh ideas for curricula more appropriate to their situations. This has been made more difficult by the inheritance of modes of examination and certification, which so concerned Ronald Dore and inspired his critique, *The Diploma Disease*. Sadly he is in a minority within the educational establishment, which at all levels tends to be an extremely conservative profession, dominated by its political masters at national, provincial and local levels. At the level of secondary schooling, this has been exacerbated by the emergence of the international comparisons of instrumental achievement, such as TIMMS and PISA, already discussed. Quite apart from issues of methodology and the fact that their tentacles, especially those of PISA, spread out to the upper echelons of the developing countries, these comparisons enhance the notion of some subjects having a higher status than others. Until such time as PISA embraces the whole curriculum and takes account of local cultural context, it will continue to be a conservative influence. It is, of course, much easier to test achievements in some subjects than others, and then compare them internationally, but at least the original International Evaluation of Achievement projects did look at areas beyond the instrumental.

The limited range of subjects currently of interest to PISA form just part of the curriculum of public schooling in the limited but expanding number of countries involved. Together, the whole of the formal curriculum, commencing at different ages in different countries and therefore exhibiting many disparities of duration, leads to the certification of a recognized qualification approximately at the end of compulsory schooling. Well-known examples are the French Baccalaureate, the English General Certificate of Secondary Education and Advanced Level General Certificate of Education, the German Abitur and the American High School Diploma. These and other examples from developed countries have a high level of international recognition that will survive migration for employment or further study. But, on a wider scale, the recognition of qualifications in an age of global mobility is a problem because of the massive range of disparities in the level of the tests involved and the methods of assessment employed. The small, mostly island, nations of the Commonwealth Caribbean have, for over forty years now, operated together through the Caribbean Examinations Council (CXC). This was made easier than it might have been due to the common legacy of the English GCE, but while keeping – indeed enhancing – the standard of that colonial inheritance, the CXC was able to make its new syllabuses more locally relevant.

The issues of standards, level and equivalence of qualifications are very sensitive internationally, and a great deal of misunderstanding is involved. Despite the long evolution of the European Union over half a century, it was quite early recognized by the governments involved in the 1953 Treaty of Rome that post-school training and the qualifications arising in technical and vocational fields offered possibilities for the migration of skilled labour. This was not the case with school-leaving qualifications such as those mentioned above, not only because of the political and social control function of formal schooling, but also because of the complex cultural identities and characteristics of the respective curricula. Now that there are twenty-seven member states the situation is even more disparate. However, Europe is leading the way in higher education through the Bologna Process. This flows from the Bologna Declaration in 1999 by twenty-nine European countries to work towards the creation of a European Higher Education Area (EHEA) to: (1) facilitate mobility of students, graduates and staff; (2) enhance student's prospects for employment, personal development and participation as citizens in democratic societies; and (3) broaden access to high-quality tertiary-level education. There are now forty-seven countries in the group who on 12 March 2010 adopted the Budapest/Vienna Declaration, thus officially launching the EHEA, extending from Iceland in the west to the Trans-Caucasian republics and eventually Kazakhstan in the east. Their aim is to agree the comparability and mutual recognition of the three cycles – bachelor's, master's and doctoral degrees – and to work together to mutual advantage with the European Cultural Convention.

In addition to the European Commission and the Council of Europe, UNESCO is also involved. This is important not only to give the Bologna Programme connections beyond its European base, but also for UNESCO to be able to use the Bologna experience to date to give some impetus to its need to grapple with the curricula and qualifications problems arising from the massive and rapid proliferation of private universities and colleges mentioned above, especially in developing countries. UNESCO has no direct power to regulate the increasingly disparate range of programmes and qualifications arising from this spate of private foundations. But it does represent the majority of the countries of the world, whose membership supports it and who are represented at a high diplomatic level. As indicated above, the emergence of private universities, especially in developing countries, is not only a result of the business community seeing a ready market. It is also due to the incapacity of governments, even in the richest countries, to fund the expansion of higher education to meet the demand. Successive higher education forums of UNESCO have focused on the problem of recognition and equivalence of qualifications at this level. UNESCO has produced principles and guidelines. To attempt to deal with the issue of the lower end of the private range, the regional scale is probably the best, and the regional offices of UNESCO are likely to have to play the leading role.

It would seem that at all levels from schooling through technical and vocational education to higher education there is a bewildering range of qualifications, the equivalence of which is very difficult to determine.

# Summary

Diversity in the formal mainstream can be a positive attribute, but dislocation disparity and dysfunctionality stand in the way of this form of education making an optimum contribution to the cooperation with non-formal and informal education that would maximize education's overall potential to address the urgent global challenges that need to be met. The mainstream 'European model' has developed from the top down, beginning with the early academic influence of the universities and churches on male-oriented schools. A close relationship with the evolution of nation states and both their emergent and full industrialization placed the national scale at the heart of decision making. As a result, little connection with local communities has developed, though the evolution of community-based schooling in the USA is one exception. The epilogue addresses the urgent question: 'Where do we go from here?' It is in the holistic approaches to responding to emergencies and to engendering sustainable development in the poor rural regions of the marginalized majority that an appropriate answer is more likely to be found.

Somehow the major systems are engulfed in internal and international competition when cooperation and collaboration are required. We need a 'cultural turn' before it is too late. A humanitarian response to educational needs everywhere can bring that about, provided we look at the potential of the global/local interface that ICT now makes possible. With that in mind communities could begin to ask the urgent question of education: where do we go from here?

# Epilogue: where do we go from here?

## Global challenges and national constraints

In order to determine the way forward with education, it is crucial that 'we start from here', that is to say 'where the learners are at'. Failing to do that, whether at the individual, classroom, whole school, national or international level, will significantly compromise the chance of success. Before we set off we need to take a long and hard look at where we are now with education, and why. Failure to do that, especially by marginalizing informal and non-formal modes of learning, is a key reason why education is a global concern. Addressing this point, and attempting to reinforce it, is what the preceding chapters have been about. The aim, especially in Chapter 2, was to establish the need to bring to bear the overarching function of education as a humanitarian response as an influence on the ingrained functions of formal education.

Although most people learn less from formal education, it is politically dominant as the tool of national governments and the multinational and international agencies they also control. Even NGOs have to operate, at least in part, under this control. So to begin with we have to remind ourselves and take into account those ingrained functions of formal education, especially schooling: it is used as a political and social control mechanism; as a vehicle for the acquisition of knowledge and skills to support national economic growth; as a selection system for allocating life paths; and as a custodial device. By marginalizing the other two forms of education, informal and non-formal, where the majority of learning actually takes place, the massive potential of education to help resolve the urgent challenges we face, including global economic crises and environmental degradation, is severely compromised.

The aims of the millennium development goals (MDGs), several concerning or relating to education in the narrow formal sense, are salutary, but the keys to unlocking the potential for education to be more effective are MDGs 7 and 8, and as such are worth repeating here:

- MDG 7: Ensure Environmental Sustainability
- MDG 8: Develop a Global Partnership for Development

These are global aspirations, and indeed necessities, for the survival of a rapidly growing human population on a finite planet spinning at 1,800 miles per hour, including an atmosphere in which we live and breath. We have nowhere else to go in the time we have to reach those two goals. Within them, two component targets should also stand out as clear priorities, namely Target 1 (T1) of MDG 7 and Target 2 (T2) of MDG 8. Again, it is worth repeating them here:

- T1 of MDG 7: get sustainable development into national policies and conserve environmental resources
- T2 of MDG 8: develop an open, rule-based, predictable non-discriminatory trading and financial system

These goals and their component targets are global and they have to be to have any credibility. Education, in all its forms and at all levels, is a necessary and probably prime actor, and will have to think globally too if it is to play its key role to good effect.

The issue of scale has been discussed above, and as illustrated in Figure 2.3, has four levels at which education operates: international, national, regional and local. Beyond international lies global, but that is not a scale at which educational decisions are likely to be made. 'Regional' is here meant to indicate areas within countries rather than groups of countries, though its other meaning, such as in the terms 'The Middle East', 'South-East Asia' or 'Europe', is also an important scale for certain issues. Crucially, under the local scale are subsumed individuals, families and communities. The two scales that matter most for maximizing chances of reaching the key goals and targets identified above are the global and the local. Global imperatives for sustainable development, based on environmental conservation and secure financial and trading practices, depend on raising the levels of learning of individuals in the localities in which they reside. This applies to all individuals and localities whether they are in affluent suburbs of Western cities or in poor rural areas of less developed countries. They will not be met by decisions at national level about school systems within which achievement in a narrow range of instrumental subjects is seen as a competition like the football Premier League. Nor will they be met by related political decisions responding to such achievements in what are seen as international competitions like the World Cup. While it is unlikely that national governments will release their grip on formal education, it does not necessarily mean that *nationalism* has to be the driving force as it is now. Indeed, it is essential that it is not.

As has been repeated deliberately as reinforcement above, the potential of education to deliver its full potential in any place depends on repairing the dislocation between the formal system and civil society wherein the non-formal and informal majority of learning takes place. This is not going to happen by chance, but the best chances are in situations where the formal system has not yet gained a nationalist grip or where it has been loosened by some kind of disaster – that is to say in the efforts of aid agencies, researchers, NGOs and local communities in the rural world of the marginalized majority and in education in emergencies. Both are constrained by national level politics and the need to recognize the contribution formal schooling can and must make, but they have the opportunity to innovate and bring the forms of education together to achieve sustainable development rather than mere reconstruction. They do not always succeed but they have the potential to do so where the formal system on its own does not. There is a great deal to be gained by the systems of developed countries from the best practices at work on the margins by such NGOs and programmes as those of ActionAid/Reflect and Practical Action (PA) described above. Family literacy programmes in the UK have also been mentioned. They, and the principles of Intermediate Technology applied at household level in this country are the kinds of initiative that need to connect with formal education. That means the generation of a new range of partnerships between all aspects of education, and between education and civil society, and most of all between politics and education.

## Partnerships: the way forward

If a much more sophisticated and thoroughgoing range of partnerships involving education does not emerge in the short and medium term, then the long-term prospects for sustainable development for all will not be realized. Education is just part of the web. At its best, through the sharing of knowledge, it can enhance the cultural capital of all, and thus increase the capacity for cooperation on a global scale.

Partnerships involving education need to be able to recognize and promote diversity as a fundamental component of sustainability. Before considering what the contrived, convoluted and compartmentalized world of formal education can learn from the more organic world of civil society, it is worth considering whether the partnerships in the natural world we call ecosystems have something to offer. Katherine Gibson et al. quote Capra's 1996 'The Web of Life' on this score:

> (t)here is no self-awareness in ecosystems, no language, no consciousness, and no culture; and therefore no justice or democracy; but also no greed or dishonesty. We cannot learn anything about those human values and shortcomings from ecosystems. But what we can and must learn from them is how to live sustainably. During more than three billion years of evolution the planet's ecosystems have organised themselves in subtle and complex ways so as to maximise sustainability.
>
> (Capra, 1996, 298, quoted in Gibson et al., 2010, 242)

They draw on this quotation in their 2010 article on 'Rethinking the Dynamics of Rural Transformation', in which they extol the virtue of economic diversity in the service of sustainable development for the rural poor of the marginalized majority of the world's population. Not only that, they go on to argue that such diversity in local economies enables them to connect more effectively with other economies, be they geographically close or remote. By contrast, the colonial practice of exploitive mono-cultural plantation economies failed to generate such mutually beneficial relationships. In relation to this they indicate that 'formal knowledge about what informally sustains rural lives and economies is largely non-existent' (245). Indeed they claim this is not without adverse effect, in that 'modern mono-cultural knowledge has actively produced the non-credibility of local ecologies of difference and presence' (ibid).

The more diversified rural economies of some developing countries have reached a level of what E.M. Schumacher, founder of Intermediate Technology, termed 'resilience', not only in economic terms, but also with regard to multifunctional communities better able to accommodate change in the form of globalization. In other words, they are able to generate and operate partnerships of various kinds and levels. Such partnerships can help to meet the challenges of the adverse effects of malnutrition, remoteness, climate change and even the current global economic crisis. Similarly, Geoff Wilson (2010) sees the need for raising the quality of the multifunctionality of poor rural communities to realize more of the potential latent in their diversity. Wilson takes the notions of economic and social capital of Bourdieu and combines them with environmental capital to form optimum multifunctionality in any given community. This is the same as resilience, the achievement of which 'is linked to dynamic changes over time associated with community learning and willingness to take responsibility and control of rural development pathways' (366).

Resilience operates at all levels from individual through household and community, drawing on all forms of education if indeed there is a school or schools to provide a formal dimension. If so, then that formal dimension needs to be a positive contributor to community learning in terms of helping to enhance all forms of capital, the totality of which is the cultural capacity referred to in Chapter 2 with regard to gender and how it can be increased in the interests of all.

If the formal dimension of education is somehow not in tune with informal and non-formal learning in relation to the economy and the environment, then the potential for enhancing the cultural capital will have been constrained by the limitations of the social capital of which formal education, where it exists, is a part. As Wilson puts it:

> the conversion of environmental and economic capital into social capital is highly dependent on power relations within a community, in particular power as an inscribed capacity to control or direct the actions of others (power possessed by an individual or group within a community), and power as a resource mobilised to achieved desired objectives within a community.
>
> (Wilson, 2010, 367)

Such disproportionate power over 'community learning', whether in the context of poor rural communities of the marginalized majority of the 'South' or in the context of the dislocated mainstream of the industrialized 'North', is the political factor controlling the provision and the content of schooling.

Partnerships within education and between education, economy, society and environment can operate at all scales from local through regional and national to international. Sustained survival on a global scale, which is what MG 7 and MG 8 are rightly aiming at, will involve interdependent development, which by definition requires partnerships. Making connections at local level must be the way forward in so-called developed societies just as in the poor rural communities mentioned above. The various forms of capital – social, economic and environmental – exist everywhere and education has a key role to play in realizing their potential for coalition in the interest of a more informed cultural capital in every locality. Meeting the challenges at the global scale, as identified by the key MDGs selected above, will come from the aggregated improvement of all localities in all countries, not by periodic global conferences dominated by national power and self-interest. Rio, Kyoto and Copenhagen are not the answer, which lies instead in the generation of educational partnerships in every locality within each of those cities, within all areas of the countries of which they are part, and likewise in all other countries, rich and poor alike.

National and local political power over education, the 'authority' that determines the extent to which the vital contribution of education can be realized, is not going to go away. Instead, that authority must itself be educated to the fact that the kind of reform required at every locality within its territory is in its own best interest. Figure 6.1 illustrates the way in which partnerships across the sectors of formal education, as well as with the non-formal and informal dimensions of learning, could be made.

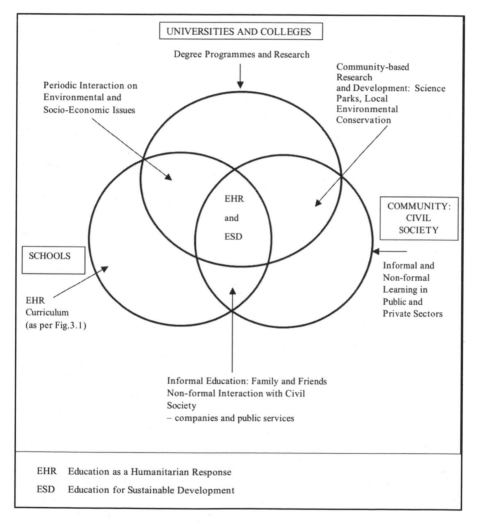

*Figure 6.1 Integrated education with locale-specific and global humanitarian and environmental sustainable perspectives*

Figure 6.1 should be considered along with Figure 3.1, above, where the components suggested for the attainment of what is termed a 'balanced humane and relevant school curriculum' are: (1) core technical expertise (literacy and numeracy and ICT) which are communication and analytical skills; (2) liberal education dimension (natural sciences, humanities and the creative and expressive arts); (3) the local resonance dimension (utilizing the local social, economic and environmental capital as far as possible as a resource through which to practise technical skills and illustrate the liberal education subject matter); (4) the informal and non-formal education of each individual to date.

Figure 6.1 takes this further, beyond the compulsory stage of formal education to develop partnerships between schools, colleges, universities and the local community in which they reside. It is at this geographical scale that the seeds of sustainable development can be sown. They will not flourish if scattered across the educational spectrum from primary to PhD with no community context in which to grow. Such growth will require a richer mix of formal, non-formal and informal learning, which can be created through the kinds of local partnership portrayed in the overlapping areas between the circles representing the different types and levels of learning that are taking place. Such an approach respects the 'authority' dimension Wilson identifies in his discussion of the maximizing of cultural capital in communities in the rural world of the marginalized majority. However, in the mainly urbanized societies of the dislocated and disparate mainstream, systems are firmly in place with their related reactionary inertia. The same would apply in large well-established towns and cities in Latin America, Asia and some of the countries of sub-Saharan Africa. But whereas in the rural majorities of less developed countries there are spaces where innovation can be introduced in the interest of enhancing cultural capacity, such as enabling greater opportunities for women and girls, such spaces are much less evident in the urban cultures of more developed countries. The overlapping areas of the circles in Figure 6.1 represent potential for the creation of spaces where greater understanding of the urgent need to address the imperatives of MDGs 6 and 7 can be fostered through partnerships between: (1) schools, colleges and universities; (2) between schools and the informal and non-formal learning in their societies and localities; (3) between universities and local societies, economies and environments.

We are talking here about creating curricular space, and between school, colleges and universities this will be a real challenge because of the so-called overcrowded curriculum. This is not likely to change because of the obsession of national political authority with the ranking of their countries on the basis of the performance of a proportion of a narrow band of their school pupils in a few subjects. Creating partnerships with universities and colleges in their area to enable their pupils to acquire some understanding of vital social, economic and environmental issues that relate directly to sustainability can enable other essential fields of study such as geology, climatology and anthropology to come into play. For obvious reasons such learning partnerships are unlikely to be permitted within normal curriculum time, but could be accommodated within vacation periods and on occasional weekend days. A good model that already exists in England is the annual Christmas science lectures for primary school pupils organized by the Royal Society, which are televised as well. For many years now, these exciting and dynamic interactive presentations have enabled a wide range of young people and adults to engage with state-of-the-art research in science. These lectures illustrate every year that, although high-level complex research is needed to extend the frontiers of scientific understanding, the results and breakthroughs are not necessarily too difficult for most children and adults to grasp if presented imaginatively.

So returning to the local community scale, it is not being suggested that every university lecturer should be involved, but there will be a few in any university who can create such presentations in cooperation with primary and secondary teachers. Unlike the Royal Society lectures mentioned above, the idea would be to consider sustainable development in the local context in periodic weekend, half-term and vacation sessions. Every location has its own geological environment, micro-climate, cultural/ multicultural community and economic situations that are capable of providing material for such sessions presented at an appropriate and participatory level for any age groups.

Such activities would attract more support if some kind of recognition or certification could be gained from participation that would gain credit towards advancing through the sectors of schooling and gaining access to further studies or employment, but not involving testing or examinations. This would go some way to alleviate Ronald Dore's concerns mentioned above, especially as the very radical innovations he suggested, though desirable, would not be likely to be accepted by political authority.

Turning to the overlap in Figure 6.1 between schools and their local community, there is considerable potential for interaction to mutual benefit. Parents, families and friends already have massive influence on the unique learning of every individual. The power of informal education is immense and not always to the good. So this is different from the partnerships that are advocated above between the sectors of formal education, in that much is happening anyway but it needs to be harnessed to the mutual benefit of schools and society. In this area of overlap, or space, connections can be made through local fieldwork with visits to schools not only by public services such as police and local councils, but also manufacturing and service industry companies, charities, religious bodies and NGOs. In the same way as international celebrities often do very important work as ambassadors for humanitarian organizations such as UNESCO and UNICEF, appropriate celebrities from any particular location could be invited to be educational ambassadors in their areas of origin. They would not have to be from the world of education itself; indeed, few would be. Most would have gained the success they have from positive human qualities such as ambition, determination, imagination, dedication and a regard for health. Luck may have played a part, but recognizing the chance if it comes along and taking it is crucial. What all this is about is taking the chance we still have to avoid environmental and economic catastrophe by responding appropriately to the challenge in every locality. In addition to representatives of elements of civil society coming into schools, pupils should also be going into local industries, public services, charities and NGOs in small groups and reporting back to create a greater accumulated understanding of the locality, its prospects and problems.

The overlap, or space, between universities and colleges and their local community is in some ways already exploited to mutual benefit, through such innovations as science and business parks, research and development projects in public health and local environmental conservation. Much depends, however, on how geographically close individual universities are to any given community. In many, perhaps most, cases there would not be a university located within the community, but more likely a tertiary college primarily providing technical and vocational education and training. Such colleges may well be connected with universities and be able to bring them into the orbit of their community. But even if they are not, they could play a useful role in partnership with civil society.

The three overlaps exhibited in Figure 6.1 do not have to operate as discrete areas for enhancing the overall educational space they have the opportunity to exploit. The overlaps intersect, which provides further opportunities for collaboration, but there is a danger of fragmentation if an overall educational network is not created. Each component of the educational community has its own organizational structure and authority structure that oversees and regulates its activities. Universities are part of a higher education sector responsible to government. Schools are responsible to local and/or national governmental authority, while civil society has its own organizations. It would be a major mistake to try to get those different authority structures to organize the kinds of partnership being suggested here. Instead, what is needed is a small 'community education committee' in each locality with representatives of the school sector, the technical/vocational sector, the university and civil society. Each member would be elected or appointed by their own sector/institution, and the committee would meet regularly. They would not so much plan, but rather stimulate educational activities in the overlaps relevant to the enhancement of social, economic and environmental capital towards sustainable development and environmental conservation. The global/local interface that has emerged as a feature of globalization through ICT will be available to enable communities in different countries to develop their own partnerships for mutual interest and development. At an international and global level, a range of important themes could be resourced for inclusion in each of the three spaces created so that learners of all ages could benefit from greater understanding. Among the top priority themes would be: (1) increased human migration and resulting multicultural societies; (2) foreign language awareness and intercultural understanding; (3) international financial and trading patterns; (4) environmental degradation and its global significance; (5) climate change; (6) the global water cycle and its fundamental significance; (7) human conflict and reconciliation; (8) natural disasters. Some of these might appear to be rather complex for consideration at school level, but in fact all could be presented imaginatively to any age group of learners. They need to be introduced during the school years for everyone in the overlaps referred to above and shared with the local community. There is, of course, already quality coverage of such issues in the printed and broadcast media but only a minority of the adult population of any country is likely to benefit from such occasional exposure.

## Conclusion

The discussion comprised in the chapters above has been based on the premise that education is a global concern, and that applying the concept of education as a humanitarian response would have some potential for allaying that concern. The extreme despair of David Orr expressed in the quotation at the beginning of Chapter 1 was that education had become obsessed with mere intellectual cleverness, rather than an attempt to understand the environment of our only home, planet Earth and how to conserve and sustain it. Such a perspective also emerged from the views of indigenous people, and the best practices of NGOs in promoting literacy from within local experience and involving intermediate technology in the service of sustainable development. The work of such NGOs, and some multinational development agencies, in response to the needs of some of the world's marginalized rural majority and those who have experienced disasters of various kinds, it has been argued, exemplifies the approach to education that is also needed to address the shortcomings of so-called developed and complete systems.

Concern is not only directed at the structures, selection procedures and curricula of most systems, but at the fact that the very nature of their being national in scale and tightly politicized makes them dysfunctional in the face of the most urgent needs expressed in the MDGs. In particular, it is suggested that MDGs 6 and 7 present the most urgent challenge, as they are concerned with ensuring environmental sustainability and creating a global partnership for development. Neither of these goals has a chance of being met while the potential of education to make its essential contribution continues to be constrained by introspective nationalistic systems in competition with each other over the attainment of a narrow band of adolescents in technical skills alone. That is precisely what David Orr had in mind by 'intellectual cleverness'. While such skills are an important component of education, they are the means of communicating, analysing and understanding information about complex human and physical environments residing in other disciplines. This may well involve, for example, the nature of human conflict and the environmental context of the location where they have occurred or are still taking place.

A recurrent underlying concern throughout this narrative has been the dislocation of the three forms of education. In this chapter, examples have been given relating to how the imperative of bringing together the forms of human capital – social, economic and environmental – is being realized in the context of some communities in the rural world of the marginalized majority. In such cases, progress is being made towards sustainable development because this inevitably involves all three forms of education, given the context. It has also been argued that global sustainable development is unlikely to be achieved by paper agreement between political leaders charged with national self-interest. The scale is just wrong, and in itself indicates why education is a global concern. Rather, the way forward is to look to the aggregation of small-scale local sustainable development in the urbanized world of the majority better-off, just as in the rural world of the majority poor.

In the context of the constipated and constrained formal systems of the mainstream, Figure 6.1 is put forward as an illustration of a way to create educational breathing spaces. These could be created by overlapping the contributions and potentials of schools, colleges universities, companies, civil society and families and indulging in a variety of imaginative interdisciplinary activities. These could be run effectively at all levels from primary school to university research projects under the aegis of a community education committee of elected representatives from educational institutions, companies, public services, local NGOs, charities and families. The knowledge and skills acquired in the type of holistic humanitarian school curriculum advocated in Figure 3.1 could then combine with the other dimensions illustrated in Figure 6.1 to educate about urgent global concerns such as climate change, the proliferation of human conflict, migration and multiculturalism, water, famine, environmental degradation, unfair trading practices and financial meltdown. All are relevant locally, some because they are evident there, others because more needs to be done by those fortunate to enjoy the everyday comforts and opportunities of development, to help support those in poverty and ill-health elsewhere. A humanitarian approach is not only suitable for disasters but should be the norm.

Modern ICT has connected the global with the local, but it has also created a digital divide between rich and poor. Despite this, as mentioned above, some aspects of this form of advanced technology can be utilized to good effect even in the poorest situations. This was illustrated in Chapter 3 with reference to the TESSA teacher education and training project. ICT can also be used to make direct links between individual schools across the globe, and there are projects already facilitating this. It needs to be extended to operate at 'community to community' level.

Education does not have to be a global concern, but it is not necessarily an automatic good, as we have seen above in relation to situations of conflict. We have the choice between the two opposing attributes of education as outlined in the quotation from Paulo Freire at the opening of Chapter 3: to use it to ensure compliance or to encourage the practice of freedom. Thus far, nations have used education to reproduce social and cultural norms. We must now urgently reject such inertia and enable people, as Freire put it, 'to discover how to participate in the transformation of their world'.

This is urgent. We need to act before the environmental tipping points of the UN Global Biodiversity Outlook of 2010 are upon us. If we operate education as a humanitarian response, that is to say in the interests of all humanity, then there is a chance that education will no longer be a global concern. If not, then it will continue to be so. The integration of formal curricula with non-formal and informal dimensions would encourage the use of imaginative and innovative cross-disciplinary contributions to knowledge, such as Gavin Pretor-Pinney's 2010 publication *The Wavewatcher's Companion*, to be more widely read. It is on the list of further reading below.

# Further Reading

Davies, Lynn (2004) *Conflict and Education: Complexity and Chaos*. London: Routledge.

Matheson, David (2008) *An Introduction to the Study of Education* (3rd edition). London: Routledge.

Phillips, David and Schweisfurth, Michele (2008) *Comparative and International Education: An Introduction to Theory, Method and Practice*. London: Continuum.

Pretor-Pinney, Gavin (2010) *Surfing the Waves of Knowledge*. London: Bloomsbury.

Retamal, Gonzalo and Aedo-Richmond, Ruth (eds) (1998) *Education as a Humanitarian Response*. London: Cassell/IBE.

Smith, Alan and Vaux, Tony (2003) *Education, Conflict and International Development*. London: DfID.

Turner, David (2004) *Theory of Education*. London: Continuum.

United Nations (2009) *Risk and Poverty in a Changing Climate*: Global Assessment Report on Disaster Risk Reduction. Geneva: UN.

# References

Abbott, Anita Trisnawatiin (2009) 'The General Agreement on Trade and Services (GATS) and Education for All (EFA): Conflict of Interest?', *Educate* 9, 2, 7–17.

Alexander, Robin (ed.) (2009) *Children, their World, their Education: Final Report and Recommendations of the Cambridge Primary Review.* Abingdon: Routledge.

Altbach, Philip, Reisberg, Liz and Rumbley, Laura E. (2009), *Trends in Global Higher Education: Tracking an Academic Revolution.* UNESCO.

Beckford, G.L. (1972) *Persistent Poverty: Underdevelopment in Plantation Economies of the Third World.* Oxford: Oxford University Press.

Bhutta, Zulfigar A. et al. (2010) 'Education of health professionals for the 21st century: a global independent Commission', *The Lancet* 375, 9721, 1137–8.

Bird, Lyndsay (2006) 'Education and Conflict: An NGO Perspective', *Forced Migration Review*, July, 30–31.

Bown, Lalage (1985) 'Without Women, No Development: The Role of Non-formal Education for Women in African Development', in Kevin Lillis (ed.), *School and Community in Less Developed Areas.* London: Croom Helm, chap. 13.

Brock, Colin and Cammish, N.K. (1997) 'Cultural Capacity-building and the Closing of the Gender Gap', in Keith Watson, Celia Modgil and Sohan Modgil, *Educational Dilemmas: Debate and Diversity, Volume Four: Quality in Education.* London: Cassell, 118–26.

Brock, Colin and Demirdjian, Lala (2010) 'The Concept of Education as a Humanitarian Response as Applied to the Arab World, with Special Reference to the Palestinian Case', in Osama Abi Mersen (ed), *Trajectories of Education in the Arab World: Legacies and Challenges.* London, Routledge and Georgetown University, 185–95.

Brown, Godfrey and Hiskett, Mervyn (eds) (1975) *Conflict and Harmony in Education in Tropical Africa.* London: Allen and Unwin.

Brun, Cathrine (2009) 'A Geographers' Imperative? Research and Action in the Aftermath of Disaster', *Geographical Journal* 175, 3, 196–207.

Buckland, Peter (2005) *Reshaping the Future: Education and Post-Conflict Reconstruction*. World Bank.

———— (2006) 'Post-conflict Education: Time for a Reality Check?', *Forced Migration Review*, special supplement on 'Education and Conflict: Research, Policy and Practice', 7–8.

Castro, Maria (2004) 'The State and the Market in the Regulation of Higher Education in Brazil', in Colin Brock and Simon Schwartzman (eds), *The Challenges of Education in Brazil*. Didcot: Symposium Books, 179–208.

Commonwealth of Learning (2009) *ICTs for Higher Education*. Paris: UNESCO, 2009).

Cremin, Lawrence (1988) *American Education: The Metropolitan Experience, 1876–1980*. New York: Harper and Row.

Davies, Lynn (2004) *Conflict and Education: Complexity and Chaos*. London: Routledge Falmer.

———— (2005) 'Schools and War: Urgent Agendas for Comparative and International Education', *Compare* 35, 4, 357–72.

Department for International Development (DfID) (2003a) *Child Labour and Its Impact on Children's Access to and Participation in Primary Education: A Case Study from Tanzania*, Research Paper No. 48, ed. H.A. Dachi and R.M. Garrett. DfID.

———— (2003b) *Researching Teacher Education: New Perspectives on Practice Performance and Policy – Multi-site Teacher Education Research Project (MUSTER) Synthesis Report*, Research Paper No. 49a, ed. Keith M. Lewin and Janet S. Stuart. London: DfID.

Dore, Ronald (1976) *The Diploma Disease*. London: Allen and Unwin.

Dyer, Caroline (2001) 'Nomads and Education for All: Education for Development or Domestication?', *Comparative Education* 37, 3, 315–27.

Freeman, Roxy (2009) 'My Gypsy Childhood', *The Guardian*, G2, 9 September.

Freire, Paulo (1970) *The Pedagogy of the Oppressed*. New York: Continuum.

Gibson, Katharine, Cahill, Amanda and McKay, Deidre (2010) 'Rethinking the Dynamics of Rural Transformation: Performing Different Development Pathways in a Philippine Municipality', *Transactions of the Institute of British Geographers: New Series* 35, 2, 237–55.

Grayling, A.C. (2001) *The Meaning of Things: Applying Philosophy to Life*. London: Weidenfeld and Nicolson.

Hargreaves, James and Boler, Tania (2006) *Girl Power: The Impact of Girl's Education on HIV and Sexual Behaviour*. Action Aid International.

Hopper, Earl (1968) 'A Typology for the Classification of Education Systems', *Sociology* 2, 29–46.

Inglis, Alex (2007) *The Educational Role of Non-Governmental Organisations in Post-Conflict Reconstruction.* MSc dissertation, University of Oxford.

International Bureau of Education (IBE) (2004) *Education, Conflict and Social Cohesion*, ed. Sobhi Tawil and Alexandra Harley. Geneva: IBE.

Joseph, Evelyn (2009) 'The Challenge of Servicing Isolated Communities', in *Pacific Educator*, Spring. Honolulu: Pacific Resources for Education and Learning (PREL).

LeVine, Robert A. and White Merry I. (1986) *Human Conditions: The Cultural Basis of Educational Developments.* New York: Kegan Paul.

Lopez-Segrera, Franciso, Brock, Colin and Dias Sobrinho, Jose (eds) (2009) *Higher Education in Latin America and The Caribbean.* Caracas: UNESCO.

McCaffery, Juliet (2009) 'Gypsies and Travellers: Literacy, Discourse and Communicative Practices', *Compare* 39, 5, 643–75.

Magger, Ole Henrik (2004) Preface, in *The Challenge of Indigenous Education: Practice and Perspectives.* UNESCO, 5–10.

Martinez, Walter Heredia (2004) 'Peru: "The Ashaninka Creators": An Experience from the Perspective of Indigenous Education', in Linda King and Sabine Schielman (eds), *The Challenge of Indigenous Education: Practice and Perspectives.* Paris: UNESCO, 205–16.

Morris, Estelle (2009) 'A Legal Right to a Good Education Doesn't Mean that You'll Get One', *The Guardian*, 24 November.

Nicolai, Susan (2007) *Fragmented Foundations: Education and Chronic Crisis in the Occupied Palestinian Territory.* UNESCO/IIEP/Save the Children.

—— (ed.) (2009) *Opportunities for Change: Education Innovation and Reform During and after Conflict.* UNESCO/IIEP.

Orr, David W. (1994) *Earth in Mind: On Education, Environment and the Human Prospect.* Washington DC: Island Press.

Oxenham, John (ed.) (1984) *Education Versus Qualifications.* London: Allen and Unwin, 1984).

Pilger, John (2006) 'Out of Eden', *The Guardian*, G2, 20 May.

Plonski, Sharri (2005) 'Developing Agency through Peace-building in the Midst of Intractable Conflict: The Case of Israel and Palestine', *Compare* 35, 4, 393–410.

Postlethwaite, T. Neville (1999) 'Overview of Issues in International Achievement Studies', in Barbara Jaworski and David Phillips (eds), *Comparing Standards Internationally: Research and Practice in Mathematics and Beyond.* Wallingford: Symposium Books, 23–60.

Ratcliffe, Richard (2007) 'The Moment of Education: The Politics of Education among the Negev Bedouin, Israel', in Colin Brock and

Lila Levers (eds), *Aspects of Education in the Middle East and North Africa*. Didcot: Symposium Books, 163–84.

Reflect (n.d.) *Reflect for ESOL Resource Pack*. Action Aid: London, http://www.skillsforlifenetwork.com/files/temp/Reflect%20for%20ESOL%20Resource%20Pack.pdf

Schaull, Richard (1972) 'Foreword', in Paulo Freire, *Pedagogy of the Oppressed*. Harmondsworth: Penguin, 13–14.

Sinclair, Margaret (2001) 'Education in Emergencies', in Jeff Crisp, Christopher Talbot and Diana B. Cipollone, *Learning for a Future: Refugee Education in Developing Countries*. Geneva: UNHCR, 1–84.

Sommers, Marc (2005) *Islands of Education: Schooling, Civil War and the Southern Sudanese (1983–2004)*. Paris: IIEP.

UNESCO ([2007] 2010a) *Education Under Attack*, ed. Brendan O'Malley. UNESCO.

UNESCO (2010b) *Protecting Education from Attack: A State-of-the Art Review*, ed. Mark Richmond. UNESCO.

UNESCO (2010c) *Reaching the Marginalized*. Oxford: UNESCO/Oxford University Press.

UNHCR (2006a) *Global Trends, Refugees, Asylum Seekers, Returnees, Displaced and Stateless Persons*. UNHCR.

—— (2006b) *Global Appeal 2006: Strategies and Programmes*. Geneva: UNHCR.

Watras, Joseph (2010) 'UNESCO's Programme of Fundamental Education, 1946–1959', *History of Education* 39, 2, 221.

Wilson, Geoff (2010) 'Multifunctional "Quality" and Rural Community Resilience', *Transactions of the Institute of British Geographers*, 35, 3 ns, 364–81.

# Index